Improvising a War

The Pentagon Years
1965-1967

Reminiscences of an
Untried Warrior

Benjamin L. Landis

Hoosick Falls, New York
2017

First published in 2017 by the Merriam Press

First Edition

Copyright © 2017 by Benjamin L. Landis
Additional material copyright of named contributors.

All rights reserved.
No part of this book may be used or reproduced in any manner whatsoever without written permission, except in the case of brief quotations embodied in critical articles or reviews.

WARNING
The unauthorized reproduction or distribution of this copyrighted work is illegal. Criminal copyright infringement, including infringement without monetary gain, is investigated by the FBI and is punishable by up to five years in federal prison and a fine of $250,000.

The views expressed are solely those of the author.

ISBN 9781576386330
Library of Congress Control Number: 2017910519

This work was designed, produced, and published in
the United States of America by the

Merriam Press
489 South Street
Hoosick Falls NY 12090

E-mail: ray@merriam-press.com
Web site: merriam-press.com

The Merriam Press publishes new manuscripts on historical subjects, especially military history and with an emphasis on World War II, as well as reprinting previously published works, including reports, documents, manuals, articles and other materials on historical topics.

Contents

Chapter 1: Preface 7
Chapter 2: Prelude 9
Chapter 3: Day One 19
Chapter 4: Day Two and Thereafter 23
Chapter 5: On My Own 31
Chapter 6: Well Diggers, Divers, Railroaders and Stevedores 39
Chapter 7: The Problems Never End 43
Chapter 8: The 9th Infantry Division 47
Chapter 9: Modified Tables of Organization and Equipment (MTOE) 55
Chapter 10: Getting the Job Done 63
Chapter 11: Senator Margaret Chase Smith 69
Chapter 12: The 196th Infantry Brigade 77
Chapter 13: Getting Organized, Finally 81
Chapter 14: The 25th Infantry Division 89
Chapter 15: The Drawdown 93
Chapter 16: Unit Readiness 101
Chapter 17: DA Versus DOD 117
Chapter 18: The Pacing Units 121
Chapter 19: The Engineer Construction Battalions 127
Chapter 20: Postlude 133
Appendix: Army Regulations 220-1 143

IN MEMORY OF
LARRY MOWERY and JOHN KISER
Gentlemen and Officers
NONE FINER

Chapter 1

Preface

THIS will be brief. The reader should not think that I have, more than forty years after the events described herein, dredged them up from an old man's memory. I first prepared these reminiscences about fifteen years after I left the Pentagon, using notes that I had written shortly after my departure as well as my still vivid memories. At the time, I thought the version was too short to be printed as a book. I, therefore, attempted to get it published as a very long article. However, the several magazines I approached were not interested. Although one editor did write that he thought they should be published, but that his magazine was not the appropriate place. I then let them gather dust in my archives during the intervening years, my time and interest taken up by other matters. It was only several months ago that I decided between other projects to edit and update the original manuscript. The result is what you are about to read.

The substance of what I wrote those many years ago has not been changed. I have made word changes. I have added or changed chapter titles. I have moved paragraphs around to give, I hope, more clarity to the story. I have made the story more personal by adding anecdotes from my own life as a career military officer. I have added a section on the Army Unit Readiness system, using for its basis the Army regulation that governed it during those years as well as my own experiences with the system. Whereas in the original manuscript I changed the names of all the persons mentioned, except those who were known to the public because of their positions, in this version I have used their real names.

All this still adds up to a short book. I, nonetheless, believe that it gives an accurate picture of how the United States Army General Staff functioned during the early and critical years of the war in Vietnam. Although the reader may not be particularly excited by how the Army General Staff worked more than forty years ago, I believe he/she will be interested in learning how the Army was caught flatfooted by the war in Vietnam and how it did its best to cope.

I hope the reading will be enjoyable, interesting, and informative.

Benjamin L. Landis
Houlgate, France
May 12, 2012

Chapter 2

Prelude

I reported for duty in the Pentagon the first week in September 1965. This was a last minute assignment. My original orders many months earlier had directed me to report to Fort Riley, Kansas, to the 1st Infantry Division. I was scheduled to be the Division G-3, Operations and Training Officer, although the final decision on my job would be the Division Commander's after my arrival. I had no reason to believe that he would not accept me as his G-3. The intended assignment was a plum for a Lieutenant Colonel, Armor, who had not always been in the good graces of those fellow officers who happened to be in charge of directing, for better or for worse, his career.

The expression "directing his career" is probably a little strong. The reality was that these officers in the Directorate of Officer Assignments were essentially preoccupied with filling officer needs throughout the Army rather than concerning themselves with guiding and managing the career of each officer in order to maximize his opportunities for advancement. And, obviously, their second concern, and sometimes, their first, was to ensure that their personal subsequent assignments were such as to maximize their own opportunities. I always remembered a conference I attended at which then Brigadier General Bruce C. Clarke declared that an officer should not allow his career to be managed by Officer Assignments, but should manage it himself. I, unfortunately, took his words to heart and made several attempts to do so. These attempts failed miserably, probably because of the maladroit way in which I made them. The efforts caused me to be ill considered by the officers who held the careers of Armor officers in their hands.

General Clarke was one of the demigods, along with General Creighton Abrams, for Armor officers of my generation, that is, the young men who started their careers at the end of the Second

World War and served during the Cold War, the Korean War, and the War in Vietnam. I first encountered him as a Brigadier General commanding the Second Constabulary Brigade in Occupied Germany. I believe that it was during this time that I heard his talk on managing one's career. He eventually acquired the four stars of a full general and finished his career as the Commander-in-Chief of the United States Army in Europe with headquarters in Heidelberg. He was, obviously, more successful at managing his career than I was in managing mine.

What had I done in trying to manage my career that had displeased the authorities in the Officer Assignment Directorate? In the spring of 1960, as my assignment in the Military Assistance Advisory Group (MAAG), France, was scheduled to end, I received orders assigning me to the 3rd Armored Cavalry Regiment stationed at Fort Meade, Maryland, to become the Operations and Training Officer (S-3) of the 3rd Squadron. Shortly after receiving these orders, I received a letter from a friend and former colleague in the Foreign Language Department of the United States Military Academy, West Point, New York, Lieutenant Colonel Sumner Willard. He advised me that the head of the department had requested my re-assignment to the department for a second 3-year tour. Sumner strongly recommended that I write to Armor Officer Assignment Division to indicate my willingness, even desire, to accept such an assignment. I was only too happy to do so.

I convinced myself that such an assignment would give me a "leg up" in becoming the Deputy Head of the Foreign Language Department upon the retirement of the current head, Colonel Barrett, and eventually the Head of the Department. I knew that a second tour would enable me to acquire a master's degree, and very possibly, a doctorate, which would further improve my chances of becoming the next Deputy Head, and subsequently, the Head.

An academic life would please me immensely. By this time in my career, after 14 years of service, after attaining the rank of major, I had lost interest in doing all the things necessary to eventually make me eligible to be designated a general officer. I wrote my letter. I received a reply that can be qualified as indignant. I believe the letter was written by Colonel Dickey, who was the head of the Armor Officer Assignment Division at that time. In summary, the letter stated that I needed additional troop duty in order to further my career and that a second assignment to the faculty at the Military Academy would be harmful to my career.

At this time I was no longer in MAAG, France, at least I was no longer working there, although still assigned there. Headquarters, United States European Command (USEUCOM, pronounced You-Ess-You-Com), then at Camp des Loges outside of Paris, had been authorized an increase in strength in its headquarters personnel, effective January 1, 1960. Instead of waiting patiently for the additional personnel to arrive from the States, the Commander-in Chief USEUCOM decided to bring in personnel from other agencies in the Paris area on Temporary Duty at no expense to the government. I was requested by name and ordered to report to Headquarters, USEUCOM, effective January 1, for temporary assignment to the Military Assistance Division. I had become well and favorably known to the officers in that Division, since it controlled and monitored all of the military assistance programs in the USEUCOM area of responsibility. I was, in short, drafted and MAAG, France, could not buck the order from its higher headquarters. I had a very interesting sojourn in USEUCOM headquarters. I was well thought of, to the point that my superiors asked if I would extend for 6 months. I was quite willing to do so. The headquarters used as one of the reasons for requesting my assignment extension the fact that my wife would be seven months pregnant at the time of my scheduled return to the United States and that it would be beneficial to the health of the prospective mother and fetus to return to the States after the child's birth.

This second effort to change my reassignment orders was met with increased indignation, even anger. The reply was to the effect that the 3rd Armored Cavalry Regiment was awaiting Major Landis and that if his pregnant wife's health was in question, he and his wife should return sooner, not later, to the United States.

I returned to the United States as scheduled. While I was on leave in Washington, D.C. my wife and I attended a cocktail party at which I encountered Colonel Dickey, the head of Armor Officer Assignment Division. He was polite, as was I. He had been the Commanding Officer of the 2nd Battalion, 14th Armored Cavalry Regiment, at Schweinfurt, Germany, when I had been in the 3rd Battalion of the same regiment at Coburg. We knew each other. He recommended that I come into the Pentagon to talk to him and his officers about my career. I was still "sulking" about his Division's thwarting my efforts to manage my career. I told him that I was too busy and had no intention of coming into the Pentagon. This did not improve my relationship with him nor with the officers who were allegedly managing my career.

The second incident that destroyed my standing with Armor Officer Assignment Branch occurred in 1963. But the story starts in 1961. The 3rd Armored Cavalry Regiment was sent to Germany in the fall of 1961 after the creation of the Berlin Wall. My first year in the regiment (July 1960-August 1961) had been very successful. I was the S-3 (Operations and Training Officer) on the staff of the 3rd Squadron. The squadron had a top notch commander, Lieutenant Colonel "Jed" Dailey. The two of us managed to achieve the highest score ever recorded by an armored cavalry squadron on its Annual Training Test (ATT), surpassing slightly the previous record set the previous year by the same squadron under the same commander with a classmate and friend of mine as the S-3.

In August 1961 I was reassigned as the Executive officer of the 2d Squadron. The new commanding officer of the squadron was Lieutenant Colonel George P. Andrews. He was undoubtedly the worst lieutenant colonel I ever encountered and could very well have been the worst lieutenant colonel in the U.S. Army at that time. None of this, of course, was immediately apparent. Troop duty in the United States was relatively undemanding. Unfortunately, the unit did not remain in the United States. In October 1961 the regiment was ordered to Germany as part of the reinforcements made because of the apprehensions of what the erection of the Berlin Wall could entail. Troop duty in Germany was demanding; it was stressful; it was competitive. Lieutenant Colonel Andrews did not understand this change in environment. Listing the errors he committed would be lengthy and tedious. Suffice it to say, it became apparent very soon after the squadron's arrival that he was first, incompetent, incapable of commanding an armored cavalry squadron, unwilling to accept the more rigid requirements of troop duty in the U.S. Army in Germany. He kowtowed to his subordinate commanders; he was totally ineffectual. But most seriously he was dishonest and a liar. Whenever the regimental commander brought to his attention an error of commission or omission, Lieutenant Colonel Andrews placed the blame on me, his deputy, or the S-3.

For the S-3 and me this was a particularly trying period. We felt very much isolated. Our commander consistently ignored our recommendations. If any troop commander complained to him about any of our instructions or actions, he consistently countermanded them. I was becoming apprehensive about the continuation of my career, about my chances for promotion. The regimental commander and executive officer did not reach out to the S-3 and me to try to ameliorate the situation. I decided after several months that I needed to get a transfer to another unit or headquarters. I had a contact in the Office of the G-1 (Personnel) at Headquarters, U.S. Army Europe (USAREUR, pronounced Yousse-A-Rur). Unfortunately, he was unable to help me get reassigned. I did not feel that I could apply for a transfer. This would have entailed an explanation of my reason for the request. On the one hand, I was uncomfortable about telling the regimental commander the true reason. I had no indications that he had any inkling of the situation in his 2d Squadron. On the other hand, I couldn't devise any spurious reason that would not be badly accepted by the regimental commander and thus influence his annual evaluation of my performance.

Then early in 1962 I came up with the idea of requesting a transfer to the newly created Intelligence Branch. A career in Intelligence without there being an Intelligence Branch was largely the domain of Reserve officers. No regular Army officer wanted to have successive tours of duty in Intelligence. No Regular Army officer's branch would permit him to have repetitive assignments in Intelligence. The creation of the intelligence branch changed that. The new Branch needed and wanted Regular Army officers. So, my reasoning was that if I obtained a Branch change, I could then quite legitimately request an assignment to an Intelligence position. This would not engender ill will at regiment.

I applied for a branch transfer. I obtained the transfer. I contacted my acquaintance at Headquarters, USAREUR, to ask him to find me an Intelligence position. I eventually received orders transferring me to the Combat Intelligence School at Oberammergau, Germany, as an instructor, effective October 12, 1962. My family and I moved to Oberammergau. I spent less than 3 months at the School. In November, before I had even taught my first lesson, I was called to Headquarters, USAREUR, to be interviewed for the position of Senior United States Liaison Officer to the Commander-in Chief of the French Forces in Germany, in Baden-Oos. I was offered the position and I accepted. I moved to Baden-Oos on January 10, 1963.

There was, however, now a new problem. The position called for an Armor officer, which I no longer was. I wore General Staff insignia upon reporting, so my real status was not evident. Nonetheless. I now had a personal problem. My career as an Intelligence officer had been aborted.. I was going to spend the next several years in an Armor officer position. If I remained in Intelligence I would be far behind my contemporaries in an Intelligence career. Therefore, I decided to request my return to Armor. To my horrified surprise it was rejected. I called Intelligence Officer Assignment Division in the Pentagon to complain. I learned that it was not the Intelligence Division that had refused to let me go, but Armor Division that had refused to accept my return. Apparently, this was the policy, never to allow a renegade back into the fold.

My contact at Intelligence Officer Assignment Division was quite sympathetic to my plight and said that he would try again. He succeeded. And I became an Armor officer again. I well imagined that this maneuver had not gone well with Armor officer

Assignment. Therefore, I was more than pleasantly surprised at my reassignment orders as G-3, 1st Infantry Division.

There were in early 1965 only fifteen combat divisions in the active U.S. Army. There were, therefore, only fifteen Division G-3 positions available to lieutenant colonels aspiring to advancement. In fact, there were even fewer positions available to any one lieutenant colonel, since Armor lieutenant colonels were given G-3 slots only in Armored Divisions and Mechanized Infantry Divisions, of which there were only four at that time. Infantry lieutenant colonels could aspire to the slots in the remaining divisions, which were all Infantry. Except that, of course, one had to be an experienced parachutist in order to be the G-3 of the two airborne divisions. Artillery lieutenant colonels were somewhat better off since they could hope for a G-3 assignment in either Armor or Infantry divisions.

Further reducing the chances of any particular lieutenant colonel being selected as a Division G-3 were the Majors, the "water walkers," who were being groomed for advancement ahead of their peers and ahead of many of their seniors. They were thus eligible for assignments normally the preserve of lieutenant colonels. In a nutshell, the chance of any particular lieutenant colonel becoming a Division G-3 was one in several thousand. Most officers never served in this coveted position.

The "3" position in any size unit--"S-3" in battalions, regiments, and brigades, the "S" standing for "staff," "G-3" in divisions, corps, armies, and army groups, the "G," for "general staff"-- was the most prestigious of all the staff positions. The "3" was the right hand and often times the alter ego of the commander. He frequently issued orders and instructions in the name of the commander for the operation of the unit, in certain circumstances without even prior consultation with his boss. He was privy to the commander's thinking, to his opinions, to his intentions, all of which he, the "3," had helped to form, sometimes before other staff officers, the subordinate commanders, even the deputy commander were. It was a position of influence and power. It was one of the recognized stepping stones on the climb to the stars, the rank of general. And in early 1965 someone had, for reasons unknown, pulled me off the siding where my career had been shunted and put me on the fast track again. Only a battalion command was a better assignment for a lieutenant colonel, and a successful Division G3 traditionally moved into a battalion command in the same division after a normal one-year tour as the "3."

When I first learned the news, I was certainly pleased, but also puzzled. It was impossible that the Infantry had ceded one of its few Infantry-only G-3 posts to Armor, even though I was a graduate of both the Basic and Advanced Infantry Officer Courses at The Infantry School, Fort Benning, Georgia. A letter from Armor Officer Assignment Division eliminated miracle as an explanation. The powers at the time in the U.S. Army had decided to transform the 1st Infantry Division (type: footslogging) into the 1st Mechanized Infantry Division (type: hell bent for leather), thus increasing by one the Division G-3 slots available to Armor lieutenant colonels. Almost miraculously my name had been put forth as a nominee and had received the requisite blessing of the hierarchy in Armor Officer Assignments as well as the blessing of the Commanding General (CG) of the soon-to-be 1st "Mech" Infantry Division.

As the weeks went by the assignment became more and more real in my originally dubious mind. I received a letter from the Division CG welcoming me to the division. I received the first of several letters from the major who had been appointed my sponsor. He had the responsibility of seeing that appropriate quarters were made available and that they were ready for occupancy upon my arrival. He was responsible for preparing my family and me for living at Fort Riley, for answering all our questions, for helping with the movement of our household goods, for meeting us upon our arrival, for shepherding us through the administrative processing, even for having food in our refrigerator when we walked into our quarters.

In the spring of 1965 sometime after the first letter from my sponsor, I read an article in a newspaper, possibly the Stars and Stripes, or the Paris Herald Tribune, or The New York Times, in which the reporter speculated that the 1st Infantry Division might be part of the recently decided build-up of U.S. armed forces in Vietnam. In my response to my sponsor's letter I asked him, not whether the speculation was accurate--I knew that such information would be classified at least SECRET-- but whether he would suggest that it might be advisable for me to find housing for my family at some location they might prefer to the environs of Fort Riley and to have my household goods shipped there. It was standard procedure that if a member of the military was reassigned to a station where his family could not accompany him, the family would lose its right to military quarters and would be obliged to relocate to lodgings on the civilian economy. Since I preferred that my family be installed in the vicinity of Washington, D.C., near my mother and sister, before I departed for Vietnam, rather than be obliged to move again after a brief sojourn at Fort Riley, I hoped to elicit some cooperative response from my sponsor.

The major in his next letter assured me that there was no reason for changing my original plans, that he was proceeding to arrange for my quarters, and that I should plan on bringing all my family and worldly possessions to historic Fort Riley.

This same exchange of correspondence occurred about a month later when, having obtained information again that the 1st Infantry Division was going to Vietnam, I asked the major for some sign, without disclosing SECRET information, such as, "in view of the possibility of the Division's being relocated in the next year" that I would be smart to find housing elsewhere for my family. Again my sponsor denied that he had any knowledge of any intention of shipping out the division, giving me detailed explanations of all he was doing to make my arrival as cordial and trouble free as possible. So, onward to Fort Riley!

At the appropriate time, I made arrangements to have the bulk of our household goods shipped from the depot where they had been stored for more than 3 years to Fort Riley. In July the movers came to our quarters in Baden-Oos, Germany, to pack the little we had brought with us in 1962 plus what we had acquired since and ship them to Kansas. In late July, a few days before our scheduled flight home, I received a cablegram from Armor Officer Assignments advising me that my orders had been cancelled and that I would receive new orders while I was on leave. The new orders assigning me to Headquarters, Department of the Army, i.e., the Pentagon, and further to the Office of the Deputy Chief Of Staff for Personnel (ODCSPER, pronounced: "Oh-Dess-Per") and further to the Promotion and Retention Division reached me in mid-August while I was on leave, about the same time that my stored household goods arrived at Fort Riley, Kansas. The other shipment from overseas was still en route there. I was no longer one of the select few. I was probably no longer on the fast track. As usual, no explanation was given for the change of orders. But, I certainly could surmise.

The weekend before my unsponsored arrival in the Pentagon the newspapers published the announcement that the 1st Infantry Division (type: footslogging) and the 1st Air Cavalry Division had embarked for Vietnam.

Chapter 3

Day One

ALTHOUGH unsponsored, my arrival was nonetheless expected in the Office of the Deputy Chief of Staff for Personnel (ODCSPER). After filling out some cards with my name, rank, serial number, the names and birthdates of my dependents, my home address, the person to be notified in case of emergency, I was led to my new office to meet my new boss and to learn what my new job would be. I did not, however, proceed to the Promotion and Retention Division, which was where I had been told I would be assigned. Between the telegram and my arrival, the urgent requirement either disappeared or was superseded by a more urgent requirement elsewhere.

My new office was located on the "C" Ring on the second floor. My new boss, Lieutenant Colonel John Kiser, promptly pointed out that it was one of the very few windowed Pentagon offices occupied solely by lieutenant colonels. Windowed offices were normally the prerogative of generals and their colonel assistants. There were three of us lieutenant colonels sharing the office: John, I, and a Lieutenant Colonel Richard Tallman. This latter got himself reassigned elsewhere in ODCSPER fairly soon after I arrived, to Congressional Liaison, I believe. The fourth person in the room--it was not very large despite the windows--was our secretary, Irma.

John's desk was placed diagonally across one corner on the window side; Dick Tallman's was placed at right angles to the wall at the opposite end and also on the window side. He sat with his back to the window. The view was not spectacular, a 10 or 15 yard airspace to the windowed walls of the "B" Ring. Standing at the window and looking up one could nonetheless see a sizeable rectangle of sky. Irma's desk was across from John's against the wall so that her back was to him when she was typing. My desk was pushed up against Dick's so that we sat facing each other. My back was to the door off the "C" Ring corridor. All the desk tops were covered with papers except mine. The only other feature I recall was a tall china cat sitting on its haunches. I suppose it was about two feet high. Painted a bright red, it was perched on top of a file cabinet behind John's desk. I was feeling too much the new kid on the block to comment on or to question its incongruous presence.

In the office adjoining ours, to which one gained access through an open doorway next to John's desk, was the other branch of the division. I believe it was designated the Manpower Branch, but I'm not sure. During my entire tour of duty in the Pentagon I never really learned exactly what the officers in that branch did. And beyond that office was the office of our division chief.

John Kiser was the Chief of the Readiness Branch in the Distribution and Readiness Division of the Directorate for Procurement and Distribution. His orientation on the branch and on my job was cordial, concise, and imprecise. He explained that the branch's purpose and mission were to manage and monitor those aspects of the Army's readiness system that involved the quantity and quality of the personnel assigned to combat units. He gave me a copy of Army Regulations 220-1, the readiness "Bible," of which he had authored the portions dealing with personnel. He recommended that I become thoroughly familiar with it. He explained that I was not replacing anyone, that the position I was about to occupy was a new one that he had been struggling to get authorized for some time.

I no longer remember why John felt he needed an additional staff officer in his branch. He was not an "empire builder." In fact, I learned over the next year that John was one of the most straight forward, sincere, honest, upright individuals I had ever met and that I could ever expect to meet. He believed totally in what he was doing, his motives were pure, his methods above reproach.

Events very quickly rendered moot any questions in my mind about the need for my position. John ended his orientation by telling me that he intended to bring me along slowly. He would begin circulating material to me for information, being careful not to give me more than he thought I could readily assimilate at any one time. He did not expect to give me any real work, projects to handle (In Pentagonese "projects" were normally referred to as "actions"), for several weeks. At the time, I was cowed enough in the presence of Army General Staff officers not to feel insulted at the almost explicit belittling of my capabilities. I did allow myself to wonder, but not out loud, how meaningful was the job I had fallen into, if it didn't require any real work for several weeks.

The rest of my first day passed lackadaisically. Officers, mostly majors and lieutenant colonels, came and went; some I was introduced to, some I was not. John and Dick came and went. Irma typed. I found the nearest men's room.

Looking for it reminded me of a story told by my boss when I was a French language instructor at West Point. In the days when he was in the Pentagon the restroom signs were horizontally painted on the walls of the entrance passages. One day my boss in a hurry saw only the "-MEN" of the women's restroom sign and darted in looking desperately for a urinal. After he had embarrassed himself in this way more than once he made an official written request that the signs be painted vertically. And so they were when I arrived. That, at least, is the story he told.

I had lunch with John and Dick. I read AR 220-1. John introduced me to the Division Chief, Colonel Jeffries, and to the officers in the other branch. John postponed to another day introducing me to the Director, Brigadier General Frank Izenour. Toward the end of the day John came back into the office from a meeting with Colonel Jeffries to announce a change of plans for me. Apparently, the Office of the Deputy Chief of Staff for Operations (ODCSOPS, pronounced "Oh-Dess-Ops") had decided to create an ad hoc inter-staff committee to assist it in managing the deployment of units to Vietnam. The committee had met for the first time that very day, and one of the lieutenant colonels from the other branch, Paul Ellison, had been appointed to represent ODCSPER. However, Paul had convinced his branch chief on his return that the mission of the committee fell rather within the purview of Readiness Branch than that of Manpower Branch. The branch chief took the point promptly to the division chief, who agreed, and told John--I'm quite sure over his protests-- that his branch would furnish the ODCSPER representative to the new committee.

Chapter 4

Day Two and Thereafter

SINCE both John and Dick already had work, and I had none, it was certainly logical in that regard that John designate me to be the ODCSPER "rep." On the other hand, the fact that I knew absolutely nothing about the functioning of the Army Staff in general, and ODCSPER in particular, plus the fact that I couldn't go from the parking lot to the office or from the office to the cafeteria with any degree of confidence in my ability not to get lost at least once, tended to argue against my designation. My availability persuaded John. Plus the fact that neither Dick nor he were interested in the assignment, which, I'm sure, they felt would be uninteresting and time consuming.

In order to compensate to some extent for my ignorance, John had extracted a commitment from Colonel Jeffries that Paul Ellison would accompany me to the committee meetings and tutor me on how to get the job done until he felt I could handle it myself. At the time no one believed that this particular function would occupy me full time. John still expected me to perform the job that he had requisitioned me to do. My feelings were mixed: I was happy to be getting real work right away; I was not happy that the committee was meeting at 8:15 in the morning.

The next day Paul came to my office and escorted me to the meeting. As we walked into the office of the ODCSOPS colonel in charge of the newly formed committee I began to feel more comfortable about the assignment. The colonel was none other than Jack Wagstaff, who had been my assistant boss in 1963-64 when I was the Senior U.S. Liaison Officer to the Commander-in Chief of the French Forces in Germany. Although I was the personal representative of the Commander-in-Chief of the United States Army in Europe to the Commander-in-Chief of the French Forces in Germany, for administrative and operational control I reported to the Deputy Chief of Staff for Operations. Wagstaff was his deputy.

He also seemed pleased to discover that he would be dealing with someone he knew. Besides two lieutenant colonels from his own office there were a representative from the Office of the Deputy Chief of Staff for Logistics (ODCSLOG, pronounced "Oh-Dess-Log") and one from the Office of the Assistant Chief of Staff for Force Development (OACSFOR, pronounced "Oh-Axe-For"). By the time that first meeting had ended I knew that I had a job to do. I was confident that I was going to be able to do it. I didn't, however, have the slightest idea how I was going to go about doing it.

Four major combat units had already been deployed to Vietnam: in the spring a brigade of the 101st Airborne Division from Fort Campbell, Kentucky, along with a Special Forces Group from Okinawa, and then the 1st Infantry Division and the 1st Air Cavalry Division in September.

Many more had been requested by General Westmoreland as well as hundreds of service units needed to support the fighting elements. Yet it seemed to me on that first day that the Army General Staff was only then beginning to get organized to handle the task of getting them to Vietnam in shape to perform their missions. How had the first four been handled, I wondered? Pretty much as "business as usual" I later learned. The job had been dumped into the lap of a WAC lieutenant colonel in Wagstaff's division. She had done her damnedest. She later became a brigadier general, Chief of the Women's Army Corps (WAC). Her boss, namely Wagstaff, finally realized that it was more than one person, however competent, in one part of the Army Staff could handle. The first four units were only the first drops of a deluge, and one thumb in the dike was not enough.

Wagstaff also realized that it was more than an ODCSOPS job. The way he put it was, "If I'm going to go down because of this, I'm not going alone." Wagstaff, although seemingly not embittered, was certainly disillusioned and frustrated by September 1965. As a very senior colonel he had watched other colonels who had worked for him receive their promotions to general.

He had been passed over for promotion to brigadier general at least twice. He figured he had one more chance. My surprise on seeing him that day was compounded because when he returned to the United States in 1964, he had been assigned to a position on the staff of the Joint Chiefs of Staff. I later learned that he had evaluated his situation and decided that he had no chance whatsoever of being selected for promotion if he remained there. He looked around, decided that the place to be was on the Army staff in ODCSOPS. Probably thanks to his seniority and his contacts, he was able to wangle a transfer. In September 1965 he found himself, I don't know whether by premonition or by chance, in the hottest seat in the Pentagon.

Where other officers, pushed, pulled and squeezed by the demands of the job and the desires of ambition, would have become tyrants in the same circumstances, it will always be to his credit among those who worked for and with him that he never lost his temper, he never became unreasonable, he never "passed the buck," he never lost his dignity nor abased that of others.

At the end of the first meeting all I knew was that I had received a stack of telegrams (in Army jargon, "TWX's," pronounced "Twicks-Ez") from units scheduled for deployment that told of personnel problems needing solving. Wagstaff had asked that I report at the next morning's meeting what ODCSPER was doing to solve them. He had also announced that the committee would meet every morning Monday through Friday at 8:15. He had also defined for us our role. We were as a group to be responsible for ensuring that the units deploying to Vietnam left the United States combat ready, with 100% of their equipment, with 100% of their personnel, and 100% qualified to perform their missions. We were each individually responsible for ensuring that the staff element we represented did its job to meet the needs of the deploying units.

To the best of my knowledge, the idea of establishing this ad hoc committee belongs to Wagstaff. He probably had to go to his boss to ask him to intervene with his counterparts in the other staff elements—ODCSPER, OACSFOR, ODCSLOG—and to persuade them to send a permanent representative to the committee. It is certain that I never saw a directive from the Secretary of the Army or from the Chief of Staff ordering the creation of such a committee or defining its role. In the beginning it was referred to as "Wagstaff's Committee" or the "Deployments Committee" or the "DCSOPS Committee." It was only with the passage of time that it became recognized as the "Department of the Army Committee for Unit Deployments to Vietnam" and was so referred to in various intra-staff written communications.

At the end of the initial meeting I rather thought that Paul Ellison would guide me through my first day of Army General Staff work, that together we would get the answers to the problems cited in the TWX's, and that together we would report back to the committee on the morrow. He quickly disabused me. He vaguely told me the answers would be found in the Office of Personnel Operations (OPO, pronounced "Oh-Poe") and that he had other work to do. John Kiser was not happy when I told him that Paul had left me on my own. A well seasoned Pentagon staff officer, he recognized, however, that this was not an issue on which to initiate a jurisdictional dispute, "to go to the mat," in Pentagonese lingo. So he told me how to find the Enlisted Personnel Directorate in OPO.

Off I went, not at all sure I was going to be able to find my way there and back. He had given me the name of a Major Duba as, at least, an initial point of contact. I found the major in the basement of the Pentagon in a very large room crammed with desks behind which sat the proverbial "little old ladies in tennis shoes and green eye shades" amid banks of metal file cabinets. Overhead were the ducts of the heating and cooling system and the water pipes. This was the office, these were the people who kept track of all the enlisted personnel in the U. S. Army. Inside the front door in lonely military attire sat Major William Duba, looking very much harassed, obviously beleaguered.

I introduced myself and explained my purpose. He welcomed me more than warmly, almost as though I were his savior. He had been desperately trying to respond to the complaints of the deploying unit commanders about personnel shortages. He had been trying to find the people to assign to these units, but had been encountering obstacles he could not overcome on his own or was hesitant to overcome on his own. He had not been able to get guidance or aid from his immediate superiors other than a sloughing "Take care of it." Filled with a "let's get the job done" attitude inspired by Wagstaff's charge to us, I told Duba that whenever he needed guidance or instructions on what to do, or authorization to do what had to be done, he could expect to get them from me.

For the next nine months or so he and I were a team, surmounting whatever obstacles, crashing through whatever roadblocks, were put in the way of moving people into deploying units. Together we skirted, we circumvented, rules, regulations, policies, chains of command. I exceeded my authority regularly in the sense that I did not bother to ask John Kiser if I could take a certain action, knowing that he would refer it to the division chief, who would most likely refer it to the director, all of it consuming time and risking a definitive "No" to the action I contemplated taking. We did whatever we had to do to get the required people into the units deploying to Vietnam. We were not always 100% successful. We were in a bureaucratic morass that at times engulfed us. We were dealing with events that were beyond our powers to control.

When President Lyndon Johnson decided to fight a war without mobilizing the Reserves or calling up the National Guard the Army was totally unprepared and could not even forecast what its problems were going to be. I may be overly harsh in my judgment. Let me say that it is possible the Army could have forecast the problems, but it made no effort to do so. The Army hierarchy decided, quite unconsciously, I'm sure, to learn by doing. It was not an efficient technique. It engendered mistakes that had to be rectified. Unfortunately for those of us who were dealing with people as a commodity of war such an attitude meant that unnecessary turmoil and anguish were inflicted upon individuals--the officers and soldiers, both professional and drafted, of the United States Army and their families-- who deserved a more reasonable and humane treatment.

My own problems with my erstwhile assignment to the 1st Infantry Division were, I learned in the Pentagon, only the tip of a very big and very icy iceberg. The decision to send the "Big Red One" to Vietnam was classified SECRET. In principle, therefore, only those officers and enlisted men authorized access to SECRET information, certainly a minority of the personnel in the Division, could be told where their unit was going. More significantly, no wife, children, parents, girlfriend, etc., could be told. Obviously, it is not possible in a peacetime environment in the United States to prepare a unit comprising around 15,000 men and thousands of pieces of equipment to deploy overseas without anyone noticing it.

Yet the fiction of the information being SECRET was maintained until the unit actually moved, despite recommendations from ODCSPER that the classification be downgraded. The reason for the request was that under the SECRET hood nothing could be done to assist the relocation of the families prior to the deployment of the unit. With the departure of a soldier, his family living in government housing at Fort Riley lost its right to that housing. When a family is not entitled to accompany the soldier spouse and parent, the Army's regulations provide that the family can move to a location of its choice at government expense. However, in order for the appropriate agencies to make the necessary moving and transportation arrangements they need to have orders stating that the spouse and parent is being shipped out. Such orders could not be issued because of the SECRET classification. The same orders were also needed by the military families living in the communities surrounding Fort Riley if they did not wish to remain there in the absence of their soldier husbands and fathers.

The Department of Defense (DOD) refused the Army's recommendation to downgrade the information. So, on the day of a departure that was common knowledge among the military and civilians of Fort Riley who had worked for months to get the division ready to go and among the thousands of family members who had long before heard the news from their spouses and parents, the information was downgraded to UNCLASSIFIED.

The wives and mothers could finally begin trying to find out what they had to do in order to get moved by the government. Unfortunately, the husband and father was no longer there to assist the spouse and children.

The same thing was happening at Fort Benning, Georgia, with the families of the 1st Air Cavalry Division. The turmoil and the morale problems created by the unrealistic application of a SECRET classification to deployments that were impossible to keep secret did at least have the beneficial result of stimulating renewed efforts by ODCSPER to persuade DOD to approve a method that would permit the issuance of family relocation orders before the departure of the spouse and parent.

Before the next units departed, DOD blessed the Army's proposal. The technique was simple: Since the only conceivable secret element in the deployment was the destination, future family relocation orders would simply state that Sergeant So-and so/Captain So-and-So, was departing with such-and-such a unit to a location in the U.S. Army, Pacific, area of responsibility (or words to that effect. After the years that have since transpired, the substance remains clear, the actual wording has faded.). A transparent subterfuge. The rules were respected, but the reality was acknowledged, and soldiers were now able to depart for a combat zone having had the opportunity to take care of their families beforehand.

Chapter 5

On My Own

EVERY morning I would proceed to Colonel Wagstaff's office bearing the sheaf of TWX's containing the status reports of units preparing to depart for Vietnam on which I was going to report that day. Some of the TWX's I had received just the day before and had been able easily to get the answers needed. Others were days, others, more than a week, old, for which answers had not been easy to get.

Where did I get these answers? But first, what were these TWX's? As can be expected, there was an Army Regulation covering the movement of units. It was designed to handle the deliberate, unprecipitous peacetime movement of already existing, fully constituted, properly trained units. One of its underlying assumptions was that there would be only a small percentage of missing personnel and only a small percentage of missing equipment. A second assumption was that it would be a fully trained unit needing no additional training, since the number of filler personnel would not be large enough to have a deleterious effect on the capabilities of the unit. A third assumption of the regulation was that time was not of the essence, that the normal and customary leaves could be granted to the members of the unit to relocate their families, visit parents, get married, get divorced, etc.

The regulation required that almost immediately after receipt of the order to deploy, the unit commander make a report on the status of his unit specifying with precision any personnel and equipment shortages and any other problems affecting the unit's readiness to move. He made this report to his immediate superior, who passed it on to his superior, noting what he had been able to do to eliminate the shortages and overcome the problems. He in turn passed it to his superior, noting... And so it went through all the tiers to Headquarters, United States Continental

Army Command (USCONARC, pronounced "You-Ess-Con-Ark"). This was the highest level Army headquarters in the United States, just below Headquarters, U.S. Army, in the Pentagon. It had a multitude of missions and controlled virtually all the personnel and equipment in the continental United States.

When Headquarters, U.S. Army, issued orders to deploy a unit to Vietnam the orders went to the Commanding General, USCONARC, whose staff then issued orders to the next lower level, and so on, until the unit received its orders from its directly controlling headquarters. Headquarters, USCONARC, was also expected to solve the shortages and problems of the deploying units, referring to the Pentagon only those matters that were clearly beyond its prerogatives or capabilities. This was at least the expectation in the Pentagon during the early deployments.

Wagstaff and his ODCSOPS staff officers, in the parlance of the Army Staff, his "action officers," and more jargonized, his "Indians," usually did not react to the initial status report. They knew the wheels were turning. Besides, the regulations specified that there were to be at least two subsequent reports. One on the Equipment Readiness Date (ERD), arbitrarily selected to be a standard number of days before the date on which the equipment was scheduled to move to the port of embarkation. If this report reflected shortages of equipment and personnel, Wagstaff expected prompt and energetic action by us to eliminate the shortages. He also expected us to keep him regularly and fully informed as to our progress. We soon learned that the unit's status would be on the agenda of every morning's meeting until we could state that we had solved its problems one way or the other. In any case, a specified number of days before the personnel were scheduled to move to the port of embarkation, on a date designated as the Personnel Readiness Date (PRD), another, and supposedly final, report was to be dispatched. Theoretically, this report should always reflect that the unit was 100% ready to embark. Any shortages or problems reported in this TWX precipitated an emergency, a crisis. Especially since the report arrived only about 10 days before the scheduled departure date. And our constant, unbending, unchanging, assigned objective was to send units to Vietnam with 100% of their personnel, fully trained, with 100% of their equipment. It almost never happened. The rules that governed our effort made it virtually impossible to attain our objective.

Colonel Wagstaff's office was long and narrow with a window at one end, a door at the other, and a second door on one side opening into a large room where his "Indians" camped. He sat with his back to the window, his desk across the room's long axis, a small conference table pushed up against his desk like the stem of a "T." For the morning meetings we all took seats at the conference table, and his senior "Indian," Lieutenant Colonel Houston, called "Sam," of course, (I no longer remember what his true first name was.) passed out the morning's receipts of TWX's. (One of Wagstaff's branch chiefs, another colonel, came to work around 6:30 in the morning, well before any else. Wagstaff had him go to the Pentagon's communications center to pick up all the newly arrived deployment status TWX's. He would make enough copies for the committee members and pass them to "Sam" before the meeting. In this way, we had the TWX's well ahead of our superiors.) Sam would go over the new messages mentioning those problems and shortages that he knew were likely to cause us trouble or that he knew would be attracting the attention of the upper reaches of the Army hierarchy. Then he would turn to his stack of old TWX's with unresolved problems. Each of us would report on the status of our efforts to solve them. Wagstaff would interject his comments, offer suggestions, exhort us to do better. Occasionally we would take the time after dealing with the day's problems to talk about ways and means to improve the system we were trying to make work.

In the beginning, Wagstaff was looking for perfection: every problem solved, every piece of equipment in place and operational by the Equipment Readiness Date, every soldier in place, trained to do his job, by the Personnel Readiness Date, for every unit deploying to Vietnam. In the beginning we didn't think it was too much to ask for. However, Wagstaff and we very quickly realized that this perfection was beyond our human grasp. The realities of time, space, and human imperfection were beyond our powers to overcome. The "system" also defied us in the beginning, but it was a contrary element that with effort and perseverance we could and did change over time. And thus enable us to move ourselves a notch closer to our unattainable goal.

It was the mission and duty of Headquarters, USCONARC, to furnish the personnel needed to fill the Vietnam-bound units from its own resources. Even in the beginning, USCONARC found this difficult to do. In the first place, personnel requirements are expressed in terms of a soldier's rank and military specialty, i.e., the skills he acquires through specific training and through practical experience. We were, therefore, directing USCONARC to give away skills and experience it needed to perform its other missions. Initially, we permitted no deviation from the precise requirements. If a unit was authorized, but didn't have, a Sergeant First Class, Mess Sergeant, we expected USCONARC to furnish a person of that rank and military specialty. We did not, however, promise USCONARC that we would replace him with his equivalent. We didn't promise to replace him at all.

USCONARC was authorized to request a replacement. The request went into the stream of all other requests from other commands and agencies for those soldiers who were available for reassignment, i.e., finishing their tour of duty overseas, finishing a period of instruction at a military specialty school, finishing their basic training, etc. USCONARC's requests did not necessarily take precedence over those from other sources, in particular, United States Army, Europe (USAREUR), and schools and agencies directly under the control of Headquarters, U.S. Army.

Headquarters, USCONARC, viewed this draining of its lifeblood rather grimly and bitterly. On the one hand, the Pentagon was asking it to take on the truly monumental task of training the flood of recruits that the increased draft calls were pulling off the streets. This meant opening new facilities, activating new units, creating new commands, all of which require people, and not just "warm bodies," but trained and experienced people. On the other hand, we were directing USCONARC to fill the units going to Vietnam with precisely those people. Headquarters,

USCONARC, contended that its training mission was as important as its duty to fill combat-bound units. Since we members of the Wagstaff committee did not have the sword to cut this Gordian knot and did not have the responsibility for staffing the recruit training centers and the other USCONARC facilities and commands, we simply insisted that our requirements be met.

The officers in the ODCSPER at Headquarters, USCONARC, solved their problem in a traditional military manner: they passed the buck back to the Pentagon whenever they had conflicting requirements. Rather than voluntarily deplete their cadre of key personnel they would notify us that they were not able to fill vacancies in deploying units from their available resources. We then had to screen all the personnel in the Army available for immediate overseas assignment to find someone. Most of the time our search would pick out the same people Headquarters, USCONARC, was trying to keep. Major Duba would have orders issued for their assignment to various deploying units. Headquarters, USCONARC, would complain that they couldn't afford to lose these people. We were always very reasonable. We would tell them that they could keep any of the selected individuals for whom they could give us an equally qualified replacement. One way or the other, someone went.

Unfortunately, by the time the maneuvering had ended, and the system had functioned, we had run out of time. The Personnel Readiness Date (PRD) had come and gone. The personnel were not only not ready, but some had not even arrived. Whenever I reported problems of this sort to the committee Wagstaff obviously wanted to know what I was doing to solve them.

Invariably, I was doing one of two things. I had already directed either my accomplice Bill Duba or my counterpart at Headquarters, USCONARC, to send the individuals concerned to their new units immediately so that they would arrive, however late, before the units departed. In order to make this solution work the soldiers had considerably less than 30 days in which to relocate their families and take care of their personal affairs, even though it was U.S. Army policy to grant at least 30-days leave to individuals being assigned to units going overseas.

This was a particularly sensitive issue after the fiasco of the 1st Infantry and 1st Air Cavalry Divisions. Nonetheless, I regularly issued instructions in contravention of this policy. Duba and my USCONARC counterpart complied with them since they knew that they could pass the buck to me. I did not consult my superiors before issuing such instructions. I did not inform them of my acts afterwards. My training had taught me that personal convenience always came in second to the needs of the Army. It had also taught me that the law may be sacrosanct, but that rules and regulations are not.

Lastly, it had taught me that one must accept the responsibility for the consequences of his acts, whether they were in compliance with or contravention of the law, the rules and the regulations. I was quite prepared to defend my decisions if any superior ever challenged them. No one ever did.

If it was impossible to get these tardily selected people to their units before they embarked, I would have orders issued for them to proceed individually to Vietnam to join their units upon their arrival. Since units normally moved by sea and individual replacements by air this solution permitted us to grant more time to the soldiers involved to take care of their families and personal affairs. This solution did, however, have two serious drawbacks.

First, the individual soldier had not been able to integrate himself into or to train with his unit. Oftentimes, these people were critically needed leaders and skilled specialists. Their absence had certainly to some degree impeded the preparation of the unit to perform fully its mission. Second, since the individuals normally arrived before their units, the U.S. Army headquarters in Vietnam frequently reassigned them to fill vacancies in units already there. The original units ended up operating in Vietnam without these people. They were obliged to submit new requisitions to their new headquarters to fill their vacancies. Or to receive another early arrival destined for a unit not yet arrived and plucked off the airport tarmac.

USCONARC very quickly ran out of people. Or, at least, ran out of people it was willing to assign to deploying units. It was passing back more and more frequently to OPO, i.e., to Major Duba, the job of finding and assigning people. Bill Duba, of course, was continuing to find the people we needed mostly in USCONARC, since the other large pool of trained and experienced soldiers was off limits to us, namely, the several hundred thousand in the U.S. Army, Europe. At this moment in the Vietnam build-up, the specific instructions from the Chief of Staff were that there would be no utilization of the resources in Europe to support the effort in Southeast Asia.

Headquarters, USCONARC, had become a hindrance. Its personnel staff officers faced an irreconcilable conflict of interest. So Major Duba and I with the relieved concurrence of our USCONARC counterparts arranged to have them relieved of any responsibility for meeting the needs of deploying units. Henceforth, Major Duba's office received the requests directly, found the people, and issued the assignment orders. (Bill Duba departed for Panama in the spring of 1966 after extraordinarily conscientious and effective performance of his duties. I don't know whether he received from his superiors the recognition and the thanks that he very much deserved. Because of his efforts his replacement did not face the crises that had been his daily diet.)

Unfortunately, we had other problems that were not so easily solved. A durable one very early forced itself upon our attention. Because the Army was rapidly expanding, we were developing a large shortage of experienced soldiers. Since the President had decided not to call up the Reserves and the National Guard, 100 percent of the Army's expansion was in the form of privates and second lieutenants. You cannot assign privates fresh out of basic training to be Platoon Sergeants and First Sergeants; you cannot assign second lieutenants fresh out of college Reserve Officers Training Corps (ROTC) or Officer Candidate School (OCS) to command companies or to be battalion staff officers. The initial deployments were units already in existence needing a relatively small number of people to "top off." However, General Westmoreland's headquarters had requested hundreds of additional units, most of which had to be created. This meant a tremendous increase in the number of officers and non-commissioned officers needed, particularly in the middle-level ranks, i.e., captain, sergeant, staff sergeant. There were simply not enough of them to go around. In order to fill the continuing flood of requests we began to deviate from our quality standards. Initially we received authorization to deviate by one grade level. We could replace a Staff Sergeant with a Sergeant, or a Sergeant with a Corporal. As the demands for people continued to grow, as more and more privates and second lieutenants flowed into the Army, we had to obtain authorization to deviate by two grade levels in order to meet certain requirements. This meant putting new second lieutenants into captain positions, putting new privates into corporal positions. There were plenty of people in the Army. There simply were not enough with the requisite training and experience.

The situation was inevitable. It was also unsatisfactory. The same unsatisfactory situation existed with respect to the hundreds of skills needed. The increased number of units increased the demand for cooks, radio operators, supply clerks, automotive mechanics, radio repairmen, armorers, etc. Initially we were able to meet the required skill levels. However, we quickly ran out of experienced specialists. We were obliged to take people who had just completed courses of instruction as cooks, mechanics, radio operators, etc., who were essentially apprentices, and assign them to positions requiring experience and advanced training.

A more significant problem was created by General Westmoreland's headquarters requesting types of units that did not exist in the peacetime army. Obviously, these units needed specialists who did not exist and for whom there were no established training courses. Some of these specialists were well diggers, divers, train crewmen, railroad dispatchers, etc.

Chapter 6

Well Diggers, Divers, Railroaders, and Stevedores

I had never heard of a well digging detachment in my nineteen years of service. I quickly learned that they are small, with 2 to 4 soldiers, a sergeant in charge, and a well digging machine. U.S. Military Assistance Command, Vietnam (USMACV, pronounced "You-Ess-Mac-Vee"), General Westmoreland's command, had requested several dozen of them. There were no such units in the Army. There were no soldiers with the appropriate Military Occupational Specialty (MOS, pronounced "M-O-S"), i.e., with well digging skills. There was no training program. The need was too small to justify establishing a training program. In any case there was not enough time to think about setting one up, even temporarily. We activated the units at military posts around the country where there were Engineer units, assigned to them soldiers with basic Engineer skills, and hoped that the equipment and people would get together early enough in the States to practice well digging before they embarked.

Divers were a different story. They are found in port construction, port operating, and port terminal units. Headquarters, USMACV, had requested a large number of these units as the need grew for port facilities to handle the increasing tons of supplies and equipment arriving in support of the war. Once again, there were no such units in existence in the peacetime army. There were, however, some divers. In fact, I learned that the Army had once had its own diver training program. It had been long since closed down. The U.S. Navy still had a diver training program; the Army had a small quota in its courses. The number of trained divers in the Army fell far short of the new and expanding need. My first thought was to ask the Navy for a greatly increased quota in its courses. The Navy turned me down. They would have considered it if I had been able to offer Army funds to support an expanded program. I didn't have the time available to get a request for additional funds approved and then to wait for the Navy to develop the additional capacity.

I had no idea where and how we were going to get our divers. I lucked out. Rather, the Army lucked out. Major Fred Miller, who had replaced Dick Tallman in the Branch, returned from an Army Readiness Team visit to Fort Belvoir, Virginia, about the time the Navy turned down my request. He had discovered quite by chance an experienced Army diver in the person of a lieutenant colonel in the headquarters of the U.S. Army Engineer School. While sitting in the outer office of the Commanding General of Fort Belvoir, waiting to go in with the other members of the team for an exit briefing, Fred had noticed an unusual badge the colonel was wearing. The colonel told him it was the insignia of a Master Diver. Knowing my plight, Fred had asked the colonel what it would take to train divers. When he learned the reasons for Fred's interest, the colonel told him that he would be happy to help. He volunteered to set up an off-the-cuff training program at Fort Belvoir. He told Fred where some of the equipment from the Army's defunct program was stored; he gave the names of some experienced divers who could be instructors. If we could get the equipment moved and get the cadre assigned, he would set up and run the program. Nothing easier. I got the ODCSLOG representative on Wagstaff's Committee to have the equipment moved. I got Duba to reassign the experienced divers to positions at Fort Belvoir controlled by the lieutenant colonel. (I don't remember his name. I'm not sure I ever knew it. I suppose I talked to him several times on the telephone to set up the administrative arrangements. Like Duba, he performed a signal service for the Army that I feel certain was never properly recognized.) Since there were no funds available to run such a program I had the OACSFOR representative on the Committee station as many as possible of the newly activated port companies at Fort Belvoir. We could then set up the diver training program as a part of their unit training program. We could also send trainees of port units stationed elsewhere to these units for room and board while they were being trained as divers.

All we needed now were people to train. I directed Major Duba to request the basic training centers to screen their next graduating classes for individuals who had swum or dived competitively in high school or college, had played water polo, had listed scuba diving as a hobby, etc. We selected the ones who looked the best and assigned them to the newly activated units, all of which were either at Fort Belvoir or in fairly close proximity at posts such as Fort Meade, Maryland, and Fort Storey, Virginia. We tabbed the files of the people we didn't need this time for future use. When I left the Pentagon in August 1967 the lieutenant-colonel's diving school was still functioning. As a footnote, over 20 years later, in talking to a professional diver whom I had met by chance, I learned that a swimming or diving capability is the least of the criteria used to select potential divers. Live and learn.

The situation with respect to railroad operating personnel was somewhat better. There was still in existence a small railway detachment, a kind of historical relic, at the U.S. Army Transportation School in Fort Eustis, Virginia. The school had managed to preserve this unit as a means of maintaining a small cadre of qualified railroad operating personnel, even though the peacetime Army had no other railroad units. General Westmoreland had included a number of different kinds of railroad units: operating detachments, signal detachments, terminal detachments, etc. in his troop requests. We had created the units. Bill Duba had started assigning people to them. Unfortunately, in doing so he virtually wiped out the detachment at Fort Eustis until I intervened, after receiving an anguished appeal from the school. Instead of deploying the trained cadre we used them to train people to man the deploying units. We also used the detachment as a home for these people when they returned from Vietnam.

There were other MOS crises throughout the time of the buildup. Stevedores, I learned, are the backbone of the Port Terminal Company, just as I learned that the Port Terminal Company's primary task is to load and unload cargo. The peacetime Army had no such units. General Westmoreland needed a large number of them. Suddenly, we had to find hundreds of stevedores, a nonexistent skill in the Army. Bill Duba and I innocently figured that a strong back was the primary requisite of a basic stevedore, so we shipped to the newly activated port terminal companies soldiers fresh out of basic training. Also, for reasons unknown to me, the Army was training more soldiers to be military policemen than were needed. So we shipped the newly trained, but unneeded, military policemen to become stevedores. We soon learned from irate port terminal company commanders that stevedoring today, at least Army stevedoring, requires training in the use of machinery as well as, and possibly in lieu of, a strong back. In any case, all we could do was commiserate with them, acknowledge our ignorance, and encourage them to train the people they had rather than to hope to get people with stevedoring skills, since there were none to be had. They also complained in vain about the unhappiness of the former military policemen.

Chapter 7

The Problems Never End

ALL these problems in trying to find, not only the right quantity, but also the right quality, of people to fill Vietnam-bound units were horribly compounded by an inaccurate personnel data bank. Looking back, I can say that this was the Stone Age of computerization. The computerized enlisted personnel data bank, known as the Enhanced Enlisted Master Tape Record (EEMTR), theoretically contained the names of all the enlisted men in the U.S. Army plus other relevant information, such as, rank, MOS, assignment, etc. The reality was far removed from the theory. It required about 90 days under the best of circumstances for any event affecting the data to be entered into the EEMTR. For example, let us say a soldier broke his leg and was hospitalized on July 1, 1966. The transmittal of the news of this event through the different levels of command and across command boundaries required about 90 days until it reached the Pentagon. Hence, it was not recorded on the EEMTR until about September 30. The problem that Bill Duba and I faced was that so far as we could know on August 15 that soldier was healthy and eligible for assignment to Vietnam. Major Duba would have orders issued assigning him to a deploying unit and ordering him to report by September 15. Usually the first time we learned that the soldier was not hale and hearty was when the unit commander reported that the position had not been filled.

Duba then had to call the soldier's original unit to learn that he had been reassigned to a hospital as a patient.

"Why didn't you notify higher headquarters what had happened when you received the orders for his reassignment?"

"He wasn't assigned to our unit any longer. We sent the orders to the hospital as a matter for them to attend to."

Rather than waste time in calling the hospital to find out why they hadn't notified higher headquarters of the soldier's inability to comply with the orders, Duba would issue new instructions to assign someone else to the unit. There were occasions when he had to issue assignment instructions three times in order to fill one vacant position. By the time the third person had received his orders the unit had often already departed.

The Army Audit Agency, a sort of military equivalent of the Government Accounting Office, Congress's "governmental watchdog" agency, had conducted an audit of the EEMTR shortly before I became one of its heavy users. The report of the audit stated that at any given moment a significant percentage of the people listed on the EEMTR were no longer in the Army. I cannot today remember the exact percentage, but it was a significant one, on the order of more than 10 percent. The audit also revealed that approximately the same percentage of soldiers actually in the Army were not listed on the tape. Among those of us familiar with the report and with the EEMTR it was a standard joke that the 10 percent of the soldiers' names on the EEMTR who were no longer in the Army were nicely balanced by the 10 percent of the soldiers in the Army whose names were not on the EEMTR. Neither circumstance improved our capability of filling units with the proper people.

By the end of 1965 the United States Army was in a parlous state. President Johnson had decided that the National Guard and the Reserves would not be used to fight the war in Vietnam. This ran contrary to all the contingency planning in the Department of Defense and the Department of the Army. At the entry of the United States into the Second World War and at the outbreak of the war in Korea Presidents Roosevelt and Truman called up the National Guard and the Reserves. The consequences for the Army in not doing so for Vietnam were horrendous. The buildup was essentially staffed by draftees, officers and enlisted. This had several effects. One that had a serious impact on the condition of the Army was the necessity to train these incoming civilians. The existing basic training centers were soon bursting at the seams. There was not the time or the resources to create new basic training centers. The solution adopted was to transform combat units in the United States into training centers.

The two armored divisions at Fort Hood, Texas, received tens of thousands of draftees and needed to divert resources in order to train them at the cost of a significant deterioration of their combat capability. The same was true also of the 5th Infantry Division at Camp Carson, Colorado. The flood of trainees into Camp Carson was so great that the excess had to be switched to Fort Riley, Kansas, formerly the home of the 1st Infantry Division, along with personnel from the 5th Infantry Division to set up a separate 5th Infantry Division training center there.

And, of course, while the Department of the Army had heaped this additional burden on these divisions, it also used them as sources of personnel for filling units deploying to Vietnam.

The two airborne divisions represented the Army's strategic reserve, although one brigade of the 101st Airborne Division had been dispatched to Vietnam and a brigade of the 82d Airborne Division was in the Dominican Republic because of the recent turmoil there. These divisions furnished personnel as individual replacements to Vietnam and also to units deploying to that country. To the extent possible they were replaced by personnel returning from overseas, but oftentimes by new second lieutenants and privates.

At the end of 1965 the United States Army in Europe was still untouchable as a resource for meeting requirements in Vietnam. The specter of a Soviet trespass into Western Europe, however remote, still haunted the dreams of the leaders of the NATO nations.

Chapter 8

The 9th Infantry Division

IN the spring of 1966 the Chief of Staff of the United States Army, General Harold Johnson, decided to activate a new infantry division, rather than send another existing one to meet General Westmoreland's request. The DCSOPS and the ACSFOR had recommended the activation; the DCSPER had "non-concurred," i.e., had recommended that the division not be activated. The DCSPER's reason was elemental: there were not sufficient people of the proper grades and skills to meet the requirements of the already existing force structure. Filling a new infantry division with the correct quantity and quality of officers, non-commissioned officers, and enlisted men would simply exacerbate the shortages that already existed in the Army outside of Vietnam. General Johnson sided with the DCSOPS and the ACSFOR. He really had no choice if he wished to respect the instructions from Mr. McNamara to furnish another division to General Westmoreland.

There were no available divisions in the United States. As I mentioned above, the 5th Infantry Division, the 1st and 2nd Armored Divisions had been turned essentially into basic training centers to train the overflow of draftees that flooded the facilities and programs of the regular training centers. The 82d Airborne Division and the 101st Airborne Division, each less a brigade, represented the Army's strategic reserve. The 25th Infantry Division in Hawaii had already been designated for deployment. The only other divisions were in Europe. Presidential approval would have been needed to withdraw one of them. In the spring of 1966 it was not likely that the President would have accepted to do so, especially since the public position of the Administration was that we could meet the requirements of Vietnam without diminishing our forces in Europe. Since it was equally improbable that General Johnson would tell Mr. McNamara that the Army could not furnish another division to General Westmoreland, he had to approve the activation of the 9th.

Rubbing salt in the wound, breaking with normal staff procedures, he directed the DCSPER, instead of the ACSFOR, to issue the activation order. For the DCSPER the question was where to find the approximately 15,000 officers and enlisted men to fill the division. Since all of the Army's personnel resources were already committed to other assignments, it meant shortchanging someone. Fortunately, in the face of the enormous demand for reinforcements that General Westmoreland had requested early in 1966, and that Mr. McNamara had approved, General Johnson did finally obtain permission to "draw down" the Army's personnel in Europe, i.e., to reassign personnel in Europe even before their scheduled date for return to the United States to units scheduled to deploy to Vietnam and to replace them with personnel in lesser grades and with lesser skills. As a result, most of the trained cadre for the new division were going to be coming home from Europe for about six months before departing for Vietnam. On the other hand, the great bulk of the enlisted men were to come from the basic training centers. In particular, there were 2,000 trainees at Fort Riley, Kansas, where the 9th Infantry Division was to be formed, who were to be assigned to the division as soon as they finished their basic training. These 2,000 recruits were being given their training by personnel of the 5th Infantry Division, stationed at Camp Carson, Colorado. The activation instructions issued by the DCSPER explicitly directed the assignment of those 2,000 recruits to the new division.

A short time after the division's activation I visited Fort Riley as the ODCSPER representative on the Department of the Army Readiness Team. During our routine visits to the units and headquarters on the post I discovered to my stupefaction that the 2,000 recruits had been assigned to various garrison housekeeping units and to battalions of the 1st Division that had been left behind because they could not be used in Vietnam, namely, a tank battalion and a rocket artillery battalion. It was in my eyes a flagrant case of disregard of explicit, specific instructions and an incomprehensible failure to understand the Army's priorities. The perpetrator of this diversion of the 2,000 soldiers was the Post Commander. Yet, he was also the Commanding General of the 9th Infantry Division. This fact made the act even more bizarre: as the Post Commander he was assigning people to peacetime housekeeping chores at the expense of the unit he was going to lead into combat.

In keeping with our normal procedures, I informed the Team Chief that this matter of the unauthorized diversion would have to be mentioned during the exit briefing that he normally conducted for the commanders and staffs of the units we visited. In this instance, the Team Chief, a lieutenant colonel like myself, opted not to follow normal procedures. He told me he had no intention of telling a major general that he had disobeyed orders. He said that if I wanted to do it, he would allow me to present the ODCSPER part of the briefing. I had no other recourse than to agree to do it.

I was not comfortable with the situation. I was, in fact, extremely apprehensive and nervous. I had never before been in a position of telling a general officer that he was out of line and that he would have to respect the original instructions. I knew it had to be done. I had spent too many months trying to find the people to assign to Vietnam-bound units so that they could enter into their combat role as well staffed and as well prepared as the Army's circumstances permitted to acquiesce in the diversion of scarce personnel to very low priority units. We were forced by the many constraints of our circumstances to send units to Vietnam understaffed with respect to rank and undertrained, but we only did it after "busting our guts," bending, even breaking the rules. It was unconscionable that someone could blithely equate the needs of peacetime garrison units to those of units going too soon into combat.

At the appropriate moment in his briefing, the ODCSOPS Team Chief turned the podium over to me. I very nervously faced the Major General and one of his Assistant Division Commanders, a Brigadier General Roseborough. I remembered well General Roseborough. He had been a Colonel in charge of

Armor officer assignments in the Pentagon when I had received those first orders assigning me to the 1st Infantry Division. I had even sent him a letter to tell him that I was "quite pleased with my next assignment," explaining that "Since I have not hesitated in the past to write your office when I have been 'disgruntled' I feel it only just that I let you know when I am satisfied." I proceeded very cautiously and tactfully to explain the problem with the assignments of the 2,000 recruits. I explained that I would have to indicate in my report that they had been assigned contrary to the instructions in the activation order. I watched my listeners very closely, apprehending the worst possible reaction, waiting for general officer wrath to strike my oh!-so-vulnerable! lieutenant colonelcy. The Major General remained calm. It was as though he had not grasped the significance of my statements or had chosen to remain indifferent to them. I knew, however, that I had not been so cautious and so tactful as not to have clearly expressed myself. Brigadier General Roseborough's complexion had become purple. He appeared to be about to burst. Luckily for me, he was not the senior officer present and could not speak until and unless his boss spoke on the matter. His boss declined to defend his decision or to take me to task, although he may have made some innocuous comment to the effect "Do what you believe you have to do, Colonel." My memory only retains the fact that I was able to finish my briefing, to leave the room when all was over, and to return to Washington without having experienced any disagreeable confrontations.

Once back in the Pentagon I was relieved to learn that my bosses were just as indignant and concerned about the diversion as I was. After I had finished and submitted my routine report, they decided that a message signed by the Chief of Staff should be dispatched to the commander at Fort Riley directing him to comply with the original instructions. I prepared the proposed message, got the DCSPER's approval, got the necessary concurrences from the other Deputy Chiefs of Staff (Nothing less would do since we were asking the Chief of Staff personally to sign the message.) and delivered the message to General Johnson's office. Although the transmittal document volunteered me to brief the Chief of Staff, we all felt that the issue was clear cut and needed no clarification. In any case, no request for a briefing was made. Finally, in about a week the proposed message came back with a handwritten note from General Johnson to the DCSPER declining to sign the message on the basis that it was necessary to allow some initiative, some leeway, to the field commanders. It was not a happy moment for any of us. Even the Chief of Staff seemed not to understand the critical level to which the Army's personnel problems had climbed.

A short time later, I was notified that I would be attending a hastily called meeting of all individuals directly involved in the deployment of units to Vietnam in the office of the Vice Chief of Staff, General Creighton Abrams. General Abrams was legendary among all Army officers, but particularly among Armor officers. Having earned the rank of Brigadier General toward the end of World War II, he had lost it as the Army shrank after the war's end. In 1946 he was a Colonel on the faculty of the Armor School at Fort Knox, Kentucky. It was there that my Armor classmates first encountered him (I was an Infantry officer at the time and was at the Infantry School, Fort Benning, Georgia.). He epitomized for them the charismatic machoism of the Armor officer, inheritor of the traditions of the Indian-fighting cavalry, Guderian, Rommel, Patton. He became their role model.

I still remember that when they appeared en masse about 40 strong in early 1947 to attend some sort of a demonstration at Fort Benning, after about six months contact with Abrams, they were all trying to talk like him, they were all smoking long, fat cigars like him, they were all trying to emulate his style. In the subsequent years most of them gave up the cigars and the mannerisms. Abrams continued to smoke them, and in 20 years he had become the second ranking officer in the Army. He later succeeded General Westmoreland in Vietnam and presided over our military withdrawal. He eventually became Chief of Staff of the Army.

I had never seen the man prior to this meeting. A considerable group of us had assembled in the anteroom to his office, not knowing the reason for or the purpose of the prospective meeting. All of Wagstaff's committee were there, as were the Army Readiness project officers, and all of our bosses up the hierarchical levels to the Deputy Chiefs of Staff. We were finally invited into the office, slightly smaller than a hotel lobby, and sat ourselves upon a variety of chairs, straight backed and overstuffed, and sofas, arranged in a ragged semicircle around a ping-pong-table-sized desk, but at a respectful distance. Behind the desk, perched in a cocked-back swivel chair, in shirt sleeves, his paunch notable, was General Abrams with a long, fat cigar stuck out in his mouth. I thought on seeing him there that without the cigar he would have looked like a slightly untranquil Buddha.

When we were all seated, he began to talk about the 9th Infantry Division and the 2,000 misassigned recruits. He mentioned that he had been away when our message had been presented to the Chief of Staff. It became apparent, although he never explicitly stated it, that he did not agree with General Johnson's attitude on field commanders' prerogatives, at least with respect to impeding the combat readiness of units headed for Vietnam. He launched into a heated, emotional discourse on the need to recognize that the first and immutable priority for the U.S. Army was the support of the Vietnam effort, that no other need, no other requirement, had precedence over it. He stated that no one--I thought I heard a slightly increased emphasis when he pronounced "no one"--had the right or authority to take any action that would in any way alter that priority, that would lessen or impede the support of the effort.

He looked around the room at all of us, generals, colonels, and lieutenant colonels who had sat quite silently and, as though speaking directly to each one of us, said in measured, emphatic words that it was absolutely our duty above all others to report to him directly any act or omission of which we learned that resulted in, or could result in, the diversion of resources, human or material, that had been assigned or committed to waging the war in Vietnam. In closing he directed that another Readiness Team visit be made in the near future to check on the status of the 9th Infantry Division. He asked if anyone had any questions. No one did. The meeting was over.

I was a member of the Readiness Team that revisited the division. All of the 2,000 recruits had been reassigned to the division, although no formal instructions were ever issued by Headquarters, United States Army. I have always assumed that there must have been a telephone call from General Abrams to that division commander.

There are two footnotes to this incident, one quite trivial, one rather sad. The trivial one first. In my job prior to coming to the Pentagon, I had frequently served as a two-way translator, French to English, English to French. Over the two and a half years during which I used and developed this skill I had reached the point where I could reconstruct almost verbatim remarks lasting about three to five minutes. Since I didn't take shorthand, I had developed a technique of jotting down key words and phrases from which I would reconstruct the remarks. At the time of the Abrams meeting this skill had not yet rusted from disuse. While he was speaking I jotted down the key words and phrases.

Immediately after the meeting I prepared a memorandum for record in which I reconstructed almost word for word Abrams' instructions to those assembled. Copies of the memorandum were distributed to the attendees, but the actual readership became considerably broader. In the succeeding months in my various encounters with Army Staff officers I was frequently surprised by those who, not knowing me, used to quote my memorandum to give the impression that they had been at the meeting.

The second footnote. Because of all the shortcomings in the Army's personnel assignment system we ended up assigning more soldiers to the 9th Infantry Division than were authorized for it, so that when the Division departed, not only did it depart over strength, but it left people behind to fill up those low priority housekeeping units and those two unneeded battalions.

Chapter 9

Modified Tables of Organization and Equipment (MTOE)

MY only subsequent encounter with General Abrams occurred under similar circumstances. It took place some months later. I was wearing another hat. John Kiser having left the Pentagon in the summer of 1966, I had inherited, as the senior lieutenant colonel in the Branch, his position as Chief. For a short while I tried to handle two jobs, that of Branch Chief and that of ODCSPER representative on the Army Unit Deployment Committee. I quickly realized that it couldn't well be done. With some regret, I turned my role of deployments representative over to one of the other officers in the Branch, Major Fred Miller.

By the early fall of 1966 the crises in the Vietnam buildup were behind us. We had over the period of a year devised ad hoc a new system to cope with the policy constraints on the one hand and the ever increasing demands of the war on the other. It had been a heady, fulfilling experience. We members of the Committee felt ourselves to be more than just cogs in the Army's machine. We all deep down inside knew that we were one of the motors turning the gears. By the early fall of 1966 the engine was turning as smoothly as it could. The buildup continued, but at a slower pace. Problems continued to pop up, but the new system was ready to handle them as routine business. I was ready for a different challenge.

One of the problems that John had left me to deal with was the longstanding quarrel with OACSFOR over changes in the Army's organization. Every unit in the Army had its entitlement to a certain quantity and quality of officers, enlisted men, and equipment. For combat units, this entitlement was called a Table of Organization and Equipment (TOE); for headquarters and administrative units it was called a Table of Distribution and Allowances (TDA). In both cases, the document specified in detail how many officers and enlisted men of what ranks and of what skills were authorized to that particular unit. By adding up all the TOEs and TDAs you would obtain a sum equaling the total strength of the Army as established by the Congress. The staff officers who dealt with manpower wholesale used such sums broken out by rank and skill level to determine the Army's needs. When they cranked into the totals their factors for losses through death, disability, discharge, retirement, etc., they established the number of people who would have to be brought into the Army by the draft and by voluntary enlistment. They also established the number of soldiers who would have to be trained in the Army's hundreds of skills. For those of us who dealt with manpower at the retail level each individual TOE and TDA determined what kind of soldier we needed to assign to a specific unit to fill a specific vacancy.

The Army's leaders, however, recognized the right of field commanders to request changes in these TOEs and TDAs to fit the circumstances of their local situations. There was a continual flow of requests to the Pentagon for approval of such modifications. Each of these requested modifications represented changes in either the quantity or quality, or both, of the Army's manpower requirements. Yet the authorized format of the requested change did not indicate what the change was. The document did not read, for example, "Change TOE 7-10 to read on Line 26, 3 each, Sergeant E5, MOS 712' in lieu of 1 each Sergeant First Class E6, MOS 722." If it had read like that, the offices that were concerned with the overall requirements of the Army would have known that for the particular type of unit in question in that particular requesting command there was a requirement for 3 less Sergeants First Class with MOS 722 and for 3 more Sergeants with MOS 712. And if the requesting command were also required to specify how many units would be affected by the change, the Army staff could determine how many more soldiers would need to be trained in MOS 712 and how many fewer in MOS 722.

However, the authorized form for a submission of a Modified Table of Organization and Equipment (MTOE) simply read "Line 26, 3 each, Sergeant E5, MOS 712."

Furthermore, a request for an MTOE could delete whole categories of personnel as well as add whole categories, instead of simply swapping them. And again, without indicating how many units were impacted.

The Office of the Assistant Chief of Staff for Force Development (OACSFOR) was the Army's organizational record keeper. This office received requests by the hundreds to approve changes to the organization of units in the field. And theoretically this office tallied the pluses and minuses of these changes to produce the record of what the Army consisted in both men and equipment.

Unfortunately, the office was not doing its job.

In 1966 the processing of changes to TOEs and TDAs was manual. The OACSFOR section responsible for processing these changes was swamped. The processing delays stretched into months. The field commanders often worsened the situation by implementing the requested changes before receiving the authorization from the Department of the Army. They would then requisition personnel to fill the positions that had not yet been authorized. Sometimes OPO would discover that the people being requested were for positions not yet approved. Sometimes OPO would not discover the duplicity and would erroneously assign people.

Further adding to the problem, as a result of the very long delays in approval of MTOE requests and of the practice by requesting commands of implementing changes before their approval, commands would submit further requests for changes based on MTOE's that had not yet been approved.

It is not far-fetched to state that in 1966 the Department of the Army did not have a precise idea of the real on-the-ground organization of the Army and of the number of personnel required by rank and Military Occupational Specialty (MOS) to staff the on-the-ground organizations.

Whenever OACSFOR finally got around to approving a TOE/TDA change, they had to get the agreement of ODCSPER before the change became official. My branch was the point of contact for obtaining this agreement. We gained this dubious privilege by default. It would have been more appropriate that another office in the Procurement and Distribution Directorate be designated as the point of contact and approval. However, history determined otherwise. At one time, the OACSFOR office that had the responsibility of staffing and approving MTOE's and TDA's had been in ODCSPER. However, sometime in 1965, as I recall (It could have been earlier.) it had been shifted to OACSFOR except for one position, which ODCSPER had retained specifically to handle its responsibility for endorsing proposed MTOE and TDA changes in personnel. This position, for reasons unknown and incomprehensible to me was placed in Readiness Branch. And during my time as Chief of the branch it was filled by a very competent and conscientious civilian employee, Mae Masterson.

Before we would agree to any proposed change we needed to know what was being added to and what was being subtracted from the Army's personnel requirements both in quantity and quality. We expected to receive this information from OACSFOR. OACSFOR refused to give us this information. They contended that they had no responsibility for developing the information, that we did not need it, and that if we wanted it, we should develop it ourselves. We contended that OACSFOR had the Army Staff responsibility for maintaining up to date the record of the Army's structure, that we needed to know what the pluses and minuses were in order to adjust our personnel requirements, and that we could not develop the information ourselves because we had neither the documentation nor the people necessary to perform the task, which was not ours to perform in the first place.

We refused to agree to any proposed changes without their net effect specified. OACSFOR refused to provide it. When I say "we" I mean myself on the recommendations of Mae Masterson and the support of my hierarchical superiors. The action officers from ACSFOR would present themselves to Mae Masterson with a MTOE to be approved. Mae would ask for the information we wanted, but, of course, it was not forthcoming. Since she did not have the authority to turn away the OACSFOR action officer, she would bring him to my desk and explain the situation. I not only told the action officer 'No," but also that I would not even take him to see my boss in the hope of getting a different reaction. And Pentagon protocol was such that he could not go over my head. My boss wouldn't even talk to him unless I accompanied him. All that he could do was return to his boss and ask that he call mine in order to try to break through the impasse. The telephone call, when and if made, did not break through.

The conflict raged at the lieutenant colonel and colonel level for months. It became a major fight between two of the offices managing the Army. Because of the fight no changes to TOEs and TDAs were being approved, except those for units in and deploying to Vietnam. The already embarrassing backlog became shameful.

Why did OACSFOR refuse to furnish the information? As we attempted to resolve the dispute as the months went by, it became apparent that OACSFOR simply did not understand or believe that we were sincere in our need for the information. I wasn't sure that ODCSPER would use the information properly when we did receive it, but the logic on which our position stood was irrefutable: we could not train or furnish to units the correct number of people in the correct grades and skills unless we knew ahead of time what the Army's needs were. Since, theoretically, we knew what they were at a given point in the past we needed to know when changes occurred after that time and exactly what those changes were.

Another reason we surmised for OACSFOR's unwillingness to cooperate was the natural reluctance to do a great deal more work. In our various negotiations their representatives used to try to blackmail us by citing the deleterious effect the already excessive backlog was having on the structural soundness of the Army. They accused us of fouling up the Army's organization by our intransigence. We replied in our righteousness that if they had been doing their job properly from the beginning we would not have been in the present mess. We had no intention of being party to their fouling up the Army by agreeing to reorganizations without knowing their effect on the Army.

The final reason for OACSFOR's position was the attitude of the major general and the colonel who were directly responsible for overseeing the processing of changes to TOEs and TDAs. They contended in meetings that in their opinion the Pentagon had no right to pass judgment on the wishes of the Army's field commanders. If the four-star general commanding the Army in Europe wanted to make changes in his organizations, we had no right to intervene. He, a lowly major general, and I, an even lowlier lieutenant colonel, should not presume to tell that general that he couldn't do what he wanted to do simply because we might not have the people he needed.

The U.S. Army had a longstanding tradition of allowing field commanders a reasonable amount of freedom of action based on the sound assumption that the persons nearest to the action and responsible for its outcome usually know best what should be done. This major general simply carried the tradition to the outer limits of absurdity, allowing the field commander to run not only his own business, but also the Army's business.

The situation became finally bad enough that news of it reached the ears of the Vice Chief of Staff. General Abrams requested an immediate decision briefing for the following Sunday morning. And obviously I was to be the ODCSPER briefer.

I had problems putting the briefing together. I felt that I should devote a certain amount of time to an issue of this importance. I tried to prepare a briefing that would last about 15 to 20 minutes. I wanted to talk about the reasons for our attitude, the way the system should work, the reasons why it was not working, with examples, theoretical and actual. When I did a "dry run" for General Izenour on Friday he was not impressed. In fact, he didn't like my approach at all. He sent me back to my desk to redo it. His instructions were that I should state what our system theoretically was for processing changes to TOEs and

TDAs, how the system ideally used the information we ideally received from OACSFOR, and why we were not presently agreeing to TOE/TDA changes. Concerned, since I was going to be the "expert" facing General Abrams, I said, "General, that's only going to take about 5 minutes, even if I speak slowly." "Fine," he replied.

Sunday morning the session began with a rambling, inconclusive presentation by an OACSFOR representative. (The ODCSLOG, originally scheduled to present its system for processing TOE/TDA changes, had subsequently withdrawn. We surmised that they did not wish to risk exposing the flaws in their system to the Vice Chief. Besides, the ODCSLOG had routinely endorsed the MTOE's and TDA's presented to it by OACSFOR. ODCSPER was the obstacle.) I then stepped to the podium, introduced myself, displayed and explained my one chart that listed the half dozen or so steps in our processing, and then stated, "The system is not currently functioning because we do not have available the necessary information. Sir, this concludes my presentation."

It must have taken all of three minutes. Silence reigned.

After several lengthy seconds that seemed ten times longer, General Abrams looked at the general officers gathered around the table and asked, "Is there any reason why I should not here and now declare an immediate moratorium on all organizational changes?"

No one said anything. No one even cleared his throat. Half a very silent minute passed. General Abrams turned to me. "Is there anything more?"

"No, sir."

"The meeting is adjourned."

Several days later we learned that the OACSFOR major general and colonel had been reassigned out of the Pentagon. Shortly thereafter we were asked to agree to a message announcing to the Army a moratorium on all organizational changes. We then heard that OACSFOR had been authorized to hire additional people to sort out and process the backlog. Sometime later we were asked to agree to another message announcing that all previously submitted requests for changes to TOEs and TDAs were to be considered null and void, unless already approved by the date of the message. The message asked further that each command make a one-time, all encompassing submission of all desired organizational changes. Finally, the message instructed that each requested change be accompanied by a breakout showing the net effect of each proposed change.

Thus was the crisis resolved. In a quite traditional way. The burden of the work was passed to lower echelons. Why wasn't this simple solution adopted earlier? No headquarters likes to admit that it is not doing its job properly. But once admission of ineffectiveness has been forced there is no longer any face to save, image to preserve. One can do the hitherto unthinkable.

By the time these events occurred I was a solidly established Army General Staff Officer. I was well on my way to deserving the Army General Staff insignia, awarded only to officers who had served satisfactorily on the Headquarters, U.S. Army General Staff for at least one year. It was a silently coveted badge of professionalism, cynically dubbed the "liver patch" because of where it was worn on the uniform. I had proved my ability to function on the Army General Staff a hundred times over. I had created a wide network of friendly contacts that gave me a reputation of being able to get things done. I had earned unquestioning credibility with my peers and my superiors. In my areas of responsibility I was the acknowledged authority on the Army General Staff and recognized as such in all the major Army headquarters worldwide. It had not always been thus. My own shaky beginnings and the misfortunes of my colleagues reminded me regularly that even the most deserved laurels wither unless constantly renewed.

Chapter 10

Getting the Job Done

MY first division chief, Colonel Jeffries, wore no laurels on his forehead. He was more concerned about keeping his head than adorning it. Colonel Jeffries was quite literally frightened of Brigadier General Izenour, his boss. We staff officers had the impression that he spent most of his time finding face-saving ways of avoiding being in Izenour's presence. The general sensed this fear and seemed to relish reinforcing it whenever an occasion presented itself. The Pentagon ritual of the "chop" was the battlefield for their war of nerves.

I do not know how or when the word entered into the jargon of the Pentagon staff with the sense in which we used it. As a verb, "to chop" meant to approve the substance and the wording of a document prepared by another office on behalf of the office for which one had by position or delegation the authority to approve.

As a substantive, "chop" meant the act or the fact of approval. A "chop" was manifested by the "chopper" placing his initials at the end of the original of the document on the line opposite the name of his office.

The ritual of the chop was essential to the coordination of the decisions and acts of the Army Staff. When the OACSFOR project officer prepared a message ordering the activation of units for deployment to Vietnam he needed to decide what other offices and agencies had to bestow their approval on the message before he could have it dispatched. Since such an action involved personnel, equipment, operations, and funds, he would need, as a minimum, chops from ODCSPER, ODCSLOG, ODCSOPS, and the Office of the Comptroller of the Army. If engineer units were involved, the Office of the Chief of Engineers would also have to chop. If intelligence units were involved, the Office of the Assistant Chief of Staff for Intelligence would have to chop.

Usually the document preparer would personally carry his document, already signed by the appropriate chief in his office, through the corridors of the Pentagon from office to office to obtain the necessary chops. This was a time-consuming and often thankless task. The sign of the experienced, accomplished staff officer was his ability to get those approving initials without wasted time and effort and without hassle. The new or unskillful staff officer without personal contacts in the various offices was obliged to blunder from desk to desk until he could find someone willing to acknowledge his responsibility for bestowing the chop for his staff agency.

The document preparer preferred to get a chop while he waited. On the other hand, the action officer who was going to get the chop from his bosses oftentimes preferred to wait, either because he was busy with his own work, or because he needed to do research on the document in order to be certain that it was acceptable to his bosses, or because he needed to obtain the chops of one or more of the other sections in his office before he could ask his bosses to chop for the office as a whole, or because he had to wait for the authorized chopper to become available, or simply because he didn't particularly like the document preparer and wanted to make him sweat. The staff officer with a network of personal contacts and IOUs outstanding could usually get his chops while he waited.

Policies varied from office to office on who had chopping authority. Policies changed as people changed. Furthermore, depending on the implications and possible consequences of any particular document the chopper might have to be at the Lieutenant General (Deputy Chief of Staff) level, at the Major/Brigadier General (Director) level, at the Colonel (Division Chief) level and exceptionally, and very rarely, at the Lieutenant Colonel (Branch Chief) level. Documents prepared for the signature of the Secretary of the Army or the Chief of Staff required chops at the Lieutenant General (Deputy Chief of Staff) level.

By the time a document reached the chopping stage it was expected to have been completely coordinated. The writer was expected to have shown a draft version that had the "O.K." of his branch, and usually his division, chief to his counterparts from whose chiefs an eventual chop was going to be requested. It was at this time, among the staff officers who were the most familiar with the issues addressed in a proposed document, that all of the possible conflicts in substance and style were expected to be resolved. Where the officers concerned were not bound by parochialism, where they felt a devotion to, and a concern for, the world beyond their "turf," where their egos and their chiefs' egos did not render them immune to reality, where they understood that reciprocal back scratching kept the Pentagon "beast" purring, they were usually able to agree on a document that met the needs that created it.

Luckily, most of the officers and civilians involved in managing the Army were pragmatists. When ideology and image brushed aside pragmatism, if the contestants or ideologies were of equal vigor, the huffing and puffing could only be stilled at the highest levels of the hierarchy. Happily, these contests were not frequent. Most of the operational decisions in the management of the Army were made by Directors responsible for certain well-defined functions, such as, the Director of Manpower and Readiness, a position held during almost all of my stay in the Pentagon by Brigadier General Izenour.

Colonel Jeffries, my Division Chief, did not ever chop. We "Indians" surmised that General Izenour had stripped him of this authority because of Jeffries' manifest lack of knowledge and understanding of the significance and potential consequences of the documents presented to him for approval. Jeffries did not enjoy going to General Izenour to ask him to chop. He rarely understood what the document represented; he became tongue-tied when he tried to answer the general's questions. Perversely, the general seemed to enjoy baiting him. In order to reduce his contacts with the general to a minimum, Colonel Jeffries, therefore, made it a rule to hold all requests for chop until the end of each day. This infuriated the document preparers and their bosses. Only rarely could he be cajoled to act more promptly. He could not be circumvented.

General Izenour would not chop until his responsible Division Chief recommended approval, and in the case of Colonel Jeffries, regardless of the low level of esteem that he accorded him.

All day long Jeffries would sit at his desk looking progressively more hounded, more put upon, piling the documents to be chopped on a corner of his desk. At the selected hour he would have his secretary call the staff officers concerned. We would notify the document preparers to hurry on over. When we had assembled in the hallway outside his office he would pick up the documents and lead us to General Izenour's anteroom, where we would discover others ahead of us and hoped to find an empty chair in which to wait. It would have been nice to have been able to take a number, go back to the office to do some theoretically useful work, and return to the general's den when the number was called. It didn't work that way. If we left, we lost our place in line.

Finally, our turn would come. In we would shuffle. Izenour, looming behind his desk, would glower at us. (He was a very big man. He walked with a loping, long stride. Whenever we walked side by side on our way to a meeting I felt very much Mutt to his Jeff, even though I stand a reasonable 5'10" tall. It was impossible to walk in step with him, one of his strides equaling about one and a half of mine.) Colonel Jeffries would begin to explain the first document to be chopped in his customary barely coherent fashion. As Izenour began to throw questions at him he would become flustered and more inarticulate. He would turn to his action officer or to the document preparer to save the day.

If they were forceful and knowledgeable they could usually convince Izenour to chop. If they were not, Izenour would become more and more unpleasant to all of them, but particularly to Colonel Jeffries as the principal cause of the fiasco. After savoring their discomfiture, he would announce his refusal to approve the document until his questions were answered and ask for the next one. So it went until all the documents were either approved or rejected.

It was during the first of these afternoon sessions that I attended that I was finally introduced officially to General Izenour. I had already been at work for several weeks. John Kiser had forgotten that Izenour had not been available to greet me the day of my arrival.

I knew that I had not met him, but caught up in my new assignment I did not often think about it. Whenever it did come to mind, the moment was not appropriate to mention it to John. In addition, my nonchalant attitude toward protocol did not incite my conscience to find an appropriate time. Colonel Jeffries undoubtedly thought that the introduction had taken place. When the introduction finally occurred it was, to say the least, embarrassing to him, for the general had to discover all by himself that I was a member of his staff.

Colonel Jeffries must have asked me to explain a document we were trying to get the general to approve. I must have aroused his curiosity by using some expression such as "our policy" or "our position." The general questioned me about my status. He quickly realized that I was one of his staff officers, that I had been so for a number of weeks, that I was representing him on the DA Unit Deployments Committee, and that I had never been presented to him. When he assimilated this he lost interest in me. He proceeded to vent his indignation on the surprised, embarrassed, dismayed Colonel Jeffries. He, in turn, after we got out of Izenour's office, tried to berate me for having failed to tell either John or him that I had not been presented. Unfortunately, he sounded more hurt than wrathful. He was so unsure of himself that he didn't seem to dare to reprimand me.

My reputation in the eyes of the general did not appear to suffer at all from this lapse in protocol. For my part, I quickly discovered that he respected subordinates who knew their jobs, who could clearly and succinctly explain issues to him, and who were able to assert, defend, and get accepted the ODCSPER point of view. He not only respected them, he trusted and relied upon them. I came to feel, and afterwards always felt, a surge of pride when Izenour, faced with chopping a document, would ask me if I considered it O.K. and upon my unadorned "Yes, Sir" would chop it without further ado.

Well before General Izenour had achieved this level of confidence in me, Colonel Jeffries had departed. His replacement was a Colonel Green: short, red hair in a crew cut, energetic, just back from Vietnam. If from Jeffries I had learned the folly of fear, from Green I learned not to believe anything said, however sincerely, until it is tested.

Chapter 11

Senator Margaret Chase Smith

VERY shortly after his arrival Colonel Green assembled all of his staff officers to tell us in emphatic terms what his policies and attitudes would be. One of the statements I retained was that he expected his staff officers to speak up and to stand up for their ideas, even when they were openly contrary to his. He apparently wanted frank subordinates who, unabashed, would do their best to keep him out of trouble. I had an early occasion to test those words.

Flowing down through the administrative channels there arrived one day a series of questions, around a dozen, as I recall, posed by Senator Margaret Chase Smith of Maine. A number of them concerned people, others concerned equipment, training, funding, etc. Under normal procedures a staff action involving several different areas of responsibility would be assigned to ODCSOPS, which would sub-assign specific items to the staff offices responsible and then consolidate the individual responses into a complete and coordinated document.

This particular action had, somehow, got sidetracked into ODCSPER. When it stopped moving it was on my desk waiting for attention. I suggested to John Kiser that we try to get responsibility transferred to ODCSOPS. John did not view my suggestion with enthusiasm. He felt that, although correct procedure would have given the action to ODCSOPS, the greatest number of questions concerned personnel matters and that it was, therefore, reasonable that ODCSPER be the responsible agency. I maintained that respecting duly assigned staff responsibilities should prevail. John also felt that ODCSOPS would never accept the transfer. (The procedures in effect in the Army Staff required that once responsibility was assigned it could be transferred only if the prospective transferee volunteered to accept it, unless the issue was argued back up the hierarchy to the Secretary of the

General Staff for resolution.) I felt that I could persuade one of my colleagues in ODCSOPS to take the action.

John finally agreed, however reluctantly, to try to convince Colonel Green to let me try to transfer it. He came back with Colonel Green's refusal. I asked him if I could try convincing the colonel. I was by now stirred up by the idea that we were being forced to violate the rules by which we conducted our daily business. I think I may also have been stirred by apprehension that I had been given a task that I was not going to be able to accomplish successfully.

I was still a fairly green Army General Staff officer. I had been in the Pentagon only a few months. In this particular assignment I was being given the responsibility for the Army's reply to an influential U.S. Senator. Certainly, the document dispatched to Senator Smith would have the approval of the various Deputy Chiefs Of Staff and, probably of the Vice Chief, if not, the Chief Of Staff. Nonetheless, they could only approve what I placed before them. So I could fail if I was unable to develop answers they were willing to approve; I could also fail, and more abjectly, if I got them to approve answers that Senator Smith would find unacceptable. Such thoughts were not, however, besieging my conscious mind. It is only in retrospect that I believe they may have been lurking in the background of my attitude.

Colonel Green accepted to see me. He was not pleased to discover the purpose of my visit. As I pleaded my case I was remembering those words he had spoken at his inaugural meeting. Each time he countered one of my arguments, I thrust anew with another variant. Our dueling match abruptly ended when, losing all patience and self-control, he exploded and essentially told me in very clear terms that he was not going to authorize transfer of the action and that I had better get to work on it. It was obvious that the time had come to cease my efforts to have logic prevail. I left his office disillusioned and disappointed and went to work.

One of the facts that had been "bugging" me was the lack of time in which to prepare an appropriate response. Under normal circumstances twenty-four, chronological, not business, hours were allotted to reply to a Congressional query. In this case, because there were more than a dozen questions, seventy-two hours had been granted by the Office of the Secretary of the General Staff. Some of those precious hours had already been used up just in getting the document to me. I had expended a smidgen more in fighting to give it away.

Unfortunately, the remaining two and a fraction days were not all available to me. I had to distribute the questions that did not fall within the domain of ODCSPER to the appropriate staff offices. I had to fix deadlines for them to get their responses back to me after they had been approved by their hierarchy. I had to prepare the ODCSPER responses. After receipt of the responses from the other staff offices, I had to prepare a final, integrated document in the requisite number of copies, to include a cover sheet transmitting the document to the Chief of Staff and a proposed letter to Senator Smith for the signature of the Chief of Staff..

All that having been accomplished, I then had to take a copy of that final document to each staff office that had input information to obtain a chop. Since the document was going to the Chief of Staff the chop would have to come from the Deputy Chief of Staff for the area concerned, i.e., Operations, Logistics, Force Development, plus the Comptroller. This meant that the chopping process would have to commence at the Branch Chief level and then progress through the Division Chief level and the Director level in order to reach the Deputy Chief of Staff. This meant that I could not get an immediate chop. I had to turn over the document to the action officer concerned and give him a deadline for returning the chopped document to me. In other words, of those 2 and a fraction days before the document had to be in the Office of the Chief of Staff, almost half of that time had to be devoted to obtaining all the necessary chops and to making any changes that the various choppers could require before chopping. And some of the remaining time would ineluctably have to be given over to sleeping and eating, although, if necessary, these activities, not to mention, spending time with one's family, could be cut drastically.

Suffice it to say, the next two days were lived frenetically.

Everyone in the office lent a hand. Even Colonel Green. We did the job and did it well. Senator Smith probably never realized the stressful days she put us through and probably would not have considered her questions important enough to justify the pressures we imposed on ourselves to answer them.

Many months later Colonel Green's unexpected successor, Larry Mowery, told me that only my performance in finally putting together the replies to Senator Smith kept Colonel Green from having me transferred as a result of my attempt to get the action transferred. He was long gone by then, however. One afternoon he had an attack of some kind in his office and was wheeled away on a stretcher, never to return.

Larry Mowery was totally different from his predecessors. He had arrived in the Division as the chief of the other branch. Everyone soon learned that he was awaiting promotion to colonel and surmised that he would, once he pinned on his eagles, move to a position befitting the new rank. Colonel Green's unscheduled departure meant that Mowery could move into a colonel's position even before being promoted and without leaving us. We "Indians" were pleased to have him get the job. Nothing he did in the subsequent months up to his departure in the summer of 1967 diminished our pleasure.

One of his first acts as Division Chief was to convince General Izenour that he, the general, need not chop every single document presented to his Directorate for approval, that he, Colonel Mowery, could be trusted to chop less-than-world-shaking documents and that he could be counted on to make a sound decision on those documents that the general needed to see and approve. This was a tremendous boon for us action officers. And even more, if Mowery felt that he could not himself chop on a document, he would tell the action officer to take it himself directly to General Izenour for approval. Life became immediately more enjoyable.

He always gave the impression of being relaxed. His predecessors seemed to view each day as grim, filled with the potential for disaster. They treated each action, however routine, as immanently cataclysmic. His predecessors were never relaxed. Their tenseness in the face of each day's work was an emanation that permeated the atmosphere of the offices. We attributed Jeffries' to his unavowed recognition that he didn't really understand what was going on and to his obvious, however much unavowed, fear of Izenour. Green was around too short a time for us to discover the root causes of his tenseness. He certainly didn't appear to be afraid of his boss and seemed to know his job. Maybe it was ambition that made him tense.

I remember discovering one evening in his attaché case, left behind inadvertently in his office, his most recent efficiency report. It occurred during one of my turns as Division Security Officer. One of his duties was to ensure that no classified documents had been left unprotected on desktops, in unlocked drawers, in briefcases. When I discovered the unlocked attaché case I went through it. There was nothing classified, but there was the efficiency report. I couldn't resist reading it. It was essentially a panegyric of Colonel Green and included the quite explicit recommendation that he be promoted to the rank of general officer. I was impressed. I was also surprised at the description of his personal and professional qualities since my brief acquaintance with him had exposed none of them to me. Nonetheless, thereafter, I was sometimes able to rationalize his conduct as an effort to live up to his efficiency rating and to latch onto a general's stars.

Larry Mowery could very well have suffered the same torments as his predecessors, but he never displayed them. He exuded unwavering self-confidence, maintaining his calm in the midst of bureaucratic crises. The pressures from above, the jockeying for power and influence, stopped in his office. The only pressure we felt was that of accomplishing our jobs as efficiently and effectively as possible. He demonstrated from the beginning complete belief in our devotion to our jobs.

The highest accolade he could bestow was to call you a "professional" with all that the word connotes of competence, devotion, skill, calm under adverse conditions, determination to perform above one's capacity, and always to perform selflessly, without histrionics, with no thought of personal advantage or gain. In his world, professionals performed at their outer limits through personal pride, motivated by a personal code of conduct, not by ideals or abstractions.

He was undoubtedly ambitious, as were we all. But he never let ambition color his judgment, his decisions, his relations with his superiors and subordinates. First came the job; second could be anything as long as it didn't interfere with the job. Yet his extreme commitment to duty and devotion to the accomplishment of mission were free of fanaticism and Big Brotherism. He assumed we were professionals. He assumed we could do our jobs. He assumed we would do our jobs. He was there to support, protect, and defend us. He was the epitome of the kind of leader we needed.

It was great to work for him. You could feel the confidence he had in you. Since we were all professionals in his eyes, it was possible for us to work with a jovial, flippant attitude, feeling free to express the ironies, even the farcical elements, tucked away in even the most serious matters. A sign of the professional to him was the ability to work seriously without being grim about it.

Obviously, not all of us could unfalteringly live up to his ideal of the professional. As time went by, as each of us had his daily performance matched against Larry Mowery's ideal of the professional, some failed in his mind's eye. For them, a scarcely perceptible change occurred in their status. The assignments they received were for less important matters. They were accorded less independence in accomplishing their tasks. Their work products were more closely scrutinized. Yet nothing in Mowery's manner, in his relationship with these persons, would ever indicate that they had somehow failed. In his mind there seemed to be always the possibility that they would regain their full status of professional.

For me Larry Mowery was the ideal boss. His concept of professionalism set up harmonics in my psyche. It felt very much in tune with my West Point-inculcated sense of duty and honor as well as with the Hemingway ideal of "grace under pressure" that was for me the summons of behavioral standards. Others with axes to grind, ambitions to foster, egos to caress, were less taken by his concepts. In any case, his taking over the division meant a definite improvement in our working environment.

In addition, I must confess, I enjoyed his company. He was a handball player. I had played off and on in my cadet days as well as during my 3 years as an instructor at West Point. Although I don't remember how it came about, we began to play handball in the Pentagon Athletic Center regularly during our lunch breaks. Most frequently, he would team up with a Marine Corps lieutenant colonel by the name of Lindsey and I would have as my partner Paul Ellison, who became the other branch chief when Mowery moved up.. We began playing together well before he became Division Chief.

We played very regularly, probably as many as 3 to 4 times a week whenever I was not on the road on a Readiness Team visit.. When Mowery became the Division Chief, General Izenour was disturbed that the 3 key officers in one of his divisions were absent at the same time. But Mowery managed to convince him that there would be no diminution in the effectiveness of his division and that we were easily and quickly within reach in case of emergency. The handball court could only be reserved for one-half hour during peak periods. Added to the playing time was the dressing and showering time plus a quick egg-salad sandwich and chocolate malted milk shake in the Athletic Center snack bar after the match. In, all we were absent about an hour to an hour and a quarter.

He also enjoyed socializing with his officers. He and his wife invited all of us and our wives to parties at their home on a number of occasions. His predecessors did not do this. One bit of trivia I remember about these parties was a game that he challenged us to. He would place a full can of Coca Cola on the floor along with a book of matches. The challenge was to stand on the can with one foot (Coca Cola cans were undoubtedly made then of stronger metal than those of today.), to bend down with the other foot off the ground to pick up the book of matches, and bent over , to extract a match and light it without losing one's balance. I was one of the few who could accomplish the feat.

Colonel Mowery departed the Pentagon a short time before I did. He went to the 101st Airborne Division, where he took over the Support Command. The division subsequently deployed to Vietnam. I heard, without attempting to confirm it, that he had command of one of the combat brigades of the Division during his tour. Upon his return to the United States he was assigned to the Infantry School. Fort Benning, Georgia, I believe, as the head of one of the academic departments. I understand he retired at Fort Benning as a Colonel. In my estimation he should have been promoted to general officer rank. He certainly outshone many of the general officers I encountered during my career.

Chapter 12

The 196th Infantry Brigade

THIS brigade had been activated at Fort Devens, Massachusetts, not to go to Vietnam, but to the Dominican Republic, where U.S. troops had been sent in April 1965 to prevent civil war. Most of the troops sent came from the 82nd Airborne Division. With the dispatch of a brigade of the 101st Airborne Division to Vietnam that same spring the Army's strategic reserve had been seriously depleted. In order to achieve a partial reconstitution of this reserve, the Department of the Army activated the 196th to replace the elements of the 82nd in the Dominican Republic.

I visited the brigade at the end of January 1966 with the DA Unit Readiness Team. The only significant personnel problem was the lack of Spanish-speaking soldiers. I agreed with the Colonel commanding the brigade that in view of the brigade's peacekeeping mission there ought to be Spanish speakers throughout the unit and, particularly, in the headquarters elements. I made this recommendation in my trip report. It was adopted. The brigade headquarters told us how many were needed and in what grades and MOS. Major Duba went to work to find and assign them.

Several months later, the situation in the Dominican Republic returning to an acceptable appearance of normality more rapidly than had been expected, the decision makers decided that the elements of the 82nd Airborne could be withdrawn without being replaced. Consequently, they decided to divert the 196th to Vietnam.

Almost immediately after the decision was transmitted to the brigade commander, he telephoned me in the Pentagon. Since I had been helpful in solving a previous personnel problem, he hoped that I could help with another created by the change of destination.

He and a number of his key commanders and staff officers had just returned from Vietnam or from other assignments where they were not accompanied by their families before being assigned to the 196th. They were not required by the policies then in force to go to Vietnam before the expiration of a specified number of months. None of them had yet been back in the United States the specified time. On the other hand, according to the colonel, this group, which included staff officers and unit commanders, had talked over the situation and had unanimously decided that, since they were going to have to return eventually to Vietnam, they preferred to go together in a unit rather than later as individual replacements.

They were therefore willing to volunteer to stay with the 196th, a decision that should please the Pentagon, but they were totally unwilling to tell their wives they had volunteered. The colonel wanted to know whether I could arrange to have orders issued by Headquarters, United States Army, directing them to deploy with the unit. The request was unusual, but I told the colonel I would see what I could do. I began to walk the request up the hierarchy. Larry Mowery accepted the idea and authorized me to take it to General Izenour. He agreed to take it to the DCSPER. General Izenour finally got back to me (there had been a couple of calls in the meantime from an anxious colonel, wondering if the powers in the Pentagon were going to deign to help him, particularly since the wives were beginning to sense that something was awry) with the news that no one was going to order these officers to remain with the brigade.

The DCSPER did, however, agree to ask one of his subordinates, the Major General, Chief of the Office of Personnel Operations (OPO), to call the colonel to tell him that the DCSPER felt that it would be in the best interests of the U.S. Army for the colonel and the other officers concerned to remain with the brigade. The Chief of OPO was supposed to express this hope in such a manner that the colonel and the others could legitimately tell their wives that the Army wanted them to go with the unit.

Apparently he did his job well, because they all went to Vietnam.

I am sure that the colonel went with stars in his eyes, because the commander of an independent brigade in combat is normally a Brigadier General. He very likely thought that after this brigade command tour he would have all the necessary tickets to get him into the ranks of the Army's generals. I later learned that when he strode down the gangway from the vessel that had transported the brigade he was met by a brigadier general from Headquarters, U.S. Army Vietnam (USARV), reputedly one of General Westmoreland's "fair haired boys," who announced that he was taking command of the 196th.

The colonel was reassigned, I understand, to a staff position somewhere. I don't know if he ever got another opportunity to command a brigade. I don't know if he ever got a star. I used to wonder though what he told his wife when he got home from his second tour in Vietnam.

Of course, those Spanish-speaking soldiers whom Bill Duba had plucked out of stateside assignments and abruptly and peremptorily moved into the brigade in the name of better relations with the people of the Dominican Republic also went to Vietnam.

Chapter 13

Getting Organized, Finally

MY job was becoming more demanding as more and more units were alerted and activated for deployment. The daily incoming tide of message reports precipitated surges of activity for me. It also created a morass of record keeping. At first, I simply made notes on the messages. If a message stated that the unit was missing a Sergeant First Class, MOS 1542, I might write in the margin, "11/15 Duba says scheduled to report 12/10." I filed the messages in the numerical order of their unit designations. Not only did this system start to take up a lot of file drawer space, but there was also the problem of having to lug a large number of messages to the daily committee meetings in order to be able to answer questions.

I then adopted the idea of setting up a card file, by unit in numerical order, writing on the cards the actions taken. The advantage of this with regard to bulkiness was overcome by my inability to post the data regularly and promptly. The cards were always incomplete and out of date. All the Committee members were attempting to cope in one way or another with this overriding need to have up-to-date information. None of them were doing any better than I. Today, anyone faced with such a problem would immediately say "Computerize it." In 1965 people did not immediately think of computers when faced with a record keeping problem. Computers were then restricted in their availability within the government. They were not in common use in business and industry. Personal computers were at the science fiction stage.

Luckily, after too many harassing months, someone working with the committee did think of using computers. He broached the idea to Colonel Wagstaff, who bought it and sold it to the appropriate decision makers in the Army hierarchy. It had to be done this way, because there was a central computer facility for the Pentagon and all the desirous users had to submit requests that were then judged as to their necessity with respect to the other requests. There was a limited amount of computer capacity available and a limited amount of time to run programs.

Eventually, the first edition of a computer report entitled "Deployment Status, United States Army," but universally referred to as DEPSTAR, was published. Every week a new edition came out.

I threw away my card file and my message file. The information received in the messages was entered directly into the computer. The information I obtained and transmitted at the morning meetings was put into the computer the same day. DEPSTAR soon became the only official source of information on deploying units. Our efficiency and effectiveness as a Committee increased many fold. I no longer remember which Committee member first had the then uncustomary thought of computerizing our record keeping. I hope he got a medal for it. He deserved one.

There were other innovations in policies and procedures that we should have adopted quickly, but failed to. The fact is that we were so very busy doing our utmost to get units ready to go to Vietnam we didn't have time to think about how we could improve our efficiency or about how we could better help the deploying units. One flagrant example of this lack of foresight was the Personnel Readiness Date.

The Army Regulations governing troop movements were unsuitable for the conditions under which we were deploying units to Vietnam. These regulations assumed, first, a very deliberate sort of deployment with a long lead time between the publication of the movement orders and the actual departure. Second, they assumed that the deploying unit was fully trained with only minor shortages of personnel and equipment. Third, they assumed that the unit would be moving from a non-combat zone to a non-combat zone. The Regulations defined a Personnel Readiness Date (PRD) and an Equipment Readiness Date (ERD). These dates were prescribed for dates very shortly prior to departure. For example, 20 days before departure for the ERD and 10 days for the PRD.

The unit commander was required to make a report immediately after publication of the movement orders to advise higher headquarters of any personnel and equipment shortages. The Regulations assumed that these shortages would be minimal. Therefore, they needed only to be eliminated by the PRD or ERD, as appropriate. The Regulations required that subsequent reports were to be made after the PRD and ERD to advise on the final pre-departure status of personnel and equipment. The Regulations assumed there would no longer be any shortages cited in these reports. If, for some inexplicable, unforeseeable reasons, there were shortages, they were expected to be of such a minor nature that they would not preclude movement of the unit, particularly since it would be going into a non-combat zone. In any case, these dates were set so close to the departure date as to preclude any action to make up the shortages.

These Regulations worked reasonably well for the early deployments, such as those of the brigade of the 101st Airborne Division, the 1st Infantry Division, the 1st Air Cavalry Division, etc. These were long existing units, well trained, with relatively few personnel and equipment shortages. We very quickly ran out of existing units to send to Vietnam. We had to create units from scratch. The provisions of the Regulations were almost totally unworkable with regard to such units. Unfortunately, we continued for some months under the pressures of time to try to make them work.

Units would reach their PRD with major shortages of people and their ERD with major shortages of equipment. I, of course, took the necessary actions to have people transferred to the unit. Such last minute transfers could not reach the unit before its scheduled departure date, unless we either gave the transferees no pre-departure leave or we postponed the date of deployment. Normally we did neither.

A unit's deployment date came to us from "on high" and was, as far as we were concerned, chiseled into stone, or rather, "fixed in concrete," our expression for the immutable. Once or twice some conscientious, or maybe conscience-stricken, unit commander would recommend in his PRD report that the deployment date for his unit be postponed until the personnel or equipment shortages could be eliminated. Such a request caused problems.

The report inevitably got into the hands of the higher levels of the hierarchy. It tended to cast doubts upon the effectiveness of the people on the Army Staff responsible for preparing the unit for deployment. It should also have cast doubts on the effectiveness of the system. However, since the ingrained attitude of the military is that the right people can make any system, however defective, work, our bosses tended in these circumstances to look at us as the problem. It was also simpler and faster to attempt to correct or replace us than it was to attempt to correct the system.

Colonel Wagstaff usually got these reports ahead of anyone else in the hierarchy. His first reaction would be to convince the executive assistants of the Chief of Staff, the Secretary of the Army, and their deputies, not to give the message to their bosses until he had had a chance to try to get the situation straightened out. He would then call the unit commander to find out exactly what was bothering him. He could usually persuade the unit commander that we were all doing our best in an imperfect world, that everything would work itself out in due course, and that there was no advantage to be gained in postponing the unit's departure. If the commander could not thus be cajoled Wagstaff would try to pinpoint his "rock-bottom" requirements, the minimum that had to be done to make him withdraw his recommendation. If it was people, Wagstaff would pass the buck to me. I would dash down to the basement to see Major Duba

"Bill," I would say, "We've got the goddamn commander of this goddamn unit who won't go to Vietnam until he gets his 2 missing company first sergeants and his missing battalion operations sergeant. Can you find out where in the hell those guys are? Are they going to report? If yes, when? If no, can you get replacements there before the unit leaves? It's going in 2 weeks. I need to know today, before the shit hits the fan. O.K.?" Bill's reaction was always positive. He was happy to do the impossible as long as he could use my name to authorize any bending, twisting, or occasional breaking of the rules. He always got back to me promptly.

"Colonel," he would report, "the one first sergeant will be arriving in 3 days. He got an extension of his leave from his old unit. The other first sergeant won't be reporting, but don't worry. I've found somebody to replace him, but he hasn't got the rank. He's only a sergeant first class, but he'll volunteer to go to get a first sergeant's slot, and he'll be there in 10 days."

"Send him."

"The operations sergeant is tough. I can't get anyone there before the unit departs. I've got somebody, a master sergeant, who's due for a Vietnam tour. Camp Carson's been hiding him. They're carrying him as a recreation specialist; he's some sort of a jock. But he's really an experienced operations sergeant. He works as the post operations sergeant when he's not jock strapping. I can assign him, but he needs leave to relocate his family. Can I give him 30 days leave with orders to join his unit when it arrives in Vietnam?."

"Let's give him just 3 weeks leave to make damn sure he's there when the unit shows up."

I would report the results to Wagstaff. He would call the unit commander with the good news and convince him that his operations sergeant would be waiting for him on the dock. He would then get the word to the executive assistants so that they could attach a note to the report to the effect that "Colonel Wagstaff's committee has taken care of this problem. The unit commander has told him to consider his recommendation withdrawn. He'll confirm withdrawal in writing." End of problem with no questions asked about how we solved it; no questions asked about how well the system was functioning.

In order to overcome the problem of people missing on the PRD we resorted regularly to the procedure of sending people directly to Vietnam to join their unit upon its arrival. We really had no alternative, even though this practice had several significant deficiencies, both from a human, as well as a military, point of view. When we learned of personnel shortages on or after the PRD, we did not have the time to determine whether the missing people were only late, but en route, or were in fact not going to report for any of a multitude of reasons. We simply assumed they were not going to appear. We found a replacement, who normally could not report before the unit departed. We directed him to proceed individually to Vietnam to join his unit. Since individual replacements traveled by air they frequently arrived before their seaborne unit. The Army headquarters in Vietnam could and often did reassign the early arrival to another unit. When his original unit arrived it would report its personnel shortage to the Army headquarters and eventually get someone. Sometimes, of course, the unit wouldn't need anyone, because the person originally assigned would have shown up, late, but in time to catch the boat.

Why did we use this problem-filled procedure? So that we could truthfully report that all units deploying to Vietnam had 100% of their authorized personnel.

As time went on and as we came to rely almost totally on newly created units to meet the requirements in Vietnam, a more serious defect in the Regulations became apparent. Since these units were built from zero strength on the day of their activation by an influx of more or less trained and experienced officers and soldiers, all strangers to each other, time was needed to train them as units as well as to sharpen their individual skills. First, squads and sections had to be developed out of these groups of strangers. Then the squads and sections had to be trained in groups of three and four to function as platoons. Then groups of four to five platoons had to be trained to function together as companies. And finally the companies had to learn to work as a battalion.

All this requires time. The concept of the PRD did not offer this time to newly activated units. I finally proposed that we modify the concept of the PRD to accommodate the needs of newly activated units scheduled to deploy to Vietnam. I recommended the establishment of a Personnel On Station Date (POSD). The POSD would be the date, rather than the PRD, on which all personnel were to have joined the unit. The PRD would then become what its name implies, the date on which the personnel of the unit are ready to depart, having completed their requisite unit training.

It was easy to obtain approval of the concept, since no one wanted to argue that we should send insufficiently trained units into combat. The arguing came over the length of time to train the units. Through the ACSFOR we turned to Headquarters, USCONARC, to propose training times for all the types of units being deployed. We told them to ignore the peacetime guidelines, to analyze the needs of each type of unit, and to propose accelerated training times, eliminating conventional training not considered essential to combat in Vietnam, adding other training that was. With new training guidelines, hurriedly put together, as was everything in those months, we started using the POSD.

(The logistics people followed our lead and created an Equipment On Station Date. They were reluctant to do so, but finally acceded when it was made clear that proper training also requires that a unit's equipment be available to its personnel.)

The POSD was an immediate success as far as we in ODCSPER were concerned. Since training times stretched to several months for specialized and for large units, we now usually had time to find a second round of people to fill vacancies reported as of the POSD and have them get leave and still report in time to integrate themselves into the unit before departure.

The use of the POSD did create a problem for General Westmoreland's headquarters. The establishment of unit training times caused us to delay the departure of some units beyond the dates requested and approved. We were happy to stand on the unarguable principle that we did not intend to send inadequately trained units into combat. The headquarters in Vietnam usually implied that we could have done better if we had really tried and that our training times were longer than they needed to be. This sort of tug of war occurred over units that for reasons unknown and unexplained to us the headquarters in Vietnam considered more necessary more quickly than the other units they had requested.

Their customary attitude in such matters was that they had already postponed the date in order to get approval from the planners at Department of Defense and that they didn't feel they should be forced to accept another delay because of our after-the-fact establishment of training guidelines. On the other hand, they did not suggest that we should send, or that they would accept, inadequately trained units. They would always suggest that they expected us to do something. Usually such tussles ended in our getting Headquarters, USCONARC, and the unit commander concerned to agree to some minor compression of the training time.

Chapter 14

The 25th Infantry Division

WHEN the 25th Infantry Division, stationed in Hawaii, was selected for deployment to Vietnam it was missing 2 of its infantry battalions. OACSFOR had to issue orders to activate 2 battalions and OPO had to issue assignment orders to about 2,000 officers and soldiers to man them. We scheduled their arrival so that sufficient time would be available to organize, equip, and train them before the division departed Oahu.

One day a staff officer, a stranger to me, from ODCSOPS appeared in my office with the very confidential information that the Chief of Staff was concerned that turning 2,000 strangers into 2 combat ready battalions could delay the departure of the Division. Apparently, General Westmoreland was not happy with the approved deployment date for the 25th and was trying to get it advanced. In trying to come up with some way of appeasing General Westmoreland or, at the least, of preventing any delay, General Johnson had thought of the two infantry battalions guarding Alaska. However, in order to make a decision, he needed more information on the status of their personnel. My job was to find out the up-to-date personnel strength of these battalions and the availability of personnel already in Alaska to fill any vacancies without arousing any suspicion in the Army headquarters in Alaska as to the real reason for my curiosity.

My first reaction was that it was a trifle late to be changing the plans. The date when the 2,000 "fillers" were due in Hawaii was close enough so that most of them had already left their previous units (some of them were coming from Europe) to go on leave to visit families, to resettle wives and children, before reporting to San Francisco for air transport to Oahu. The probability of tracking them down while they were traveling was virtually nil.

Theoretically we should have been able to cull them when they reported to the San Francisco Port of Embarkation. In order to do so we would have needed to be able to identify them to the authorities at the Port by name. This we couldn't do. First, the orders for the 2000 were no different from the orders of other soldiers going to the Division to fill other vacancies. Second, some of them were coming from Europe, and we in the Pentagon had no record of who they were. Third, since the record of their assignments was not yet in the EEMTR any effort to identify the 2000 by name would have had to be done manually. There were not enough people available in USAREUR headquarters and in Major Duba's "shop" to accomplish that task, even working around the clock until they dropped, in time to stop the fillers at San Francisco. If General Johnson changed the plan, we were going to end up with a couple of thousand extra people in Hawaii, people whose lives we had disrupted for no useful purpose, and who were more useful to the Army elsewhere.

I proceeded to get the desired information. I telephoned to the G-1 at Headquarters, U.S. Army, Alaska to set up a time to talk with him via the "scrambler" phone, i.e., a telephone in the Department of the Army' situation room that encrypts telephone conversations.. At the appointed time I told him that I needed to know the personnel vacancies in the two infantry battalions in Alaska by MOS (Military Occupational Specialty) and authorized rank. I added that I also needed to know how many of the vacancies could be filled by people already in the command but assigned to other units and headquarters. I gave him as my reason for wanting the information that the Chief of Staff had ordered a detailed analysis of the readiness of all the Army's combat units outside of Vietnam.

Since I was known to be one of the Pentagon staff officers concerned with monitoring the Army's worldwide readiness status (I was not as well known outside of the Pentagon for my other role as the Pentagon's personnel manager for Vietnam deployments.) and since there was continuing press and Congressional interest in the capability of the Army to meet its commitments worldwide in the face of the diversion of resources to Southeast Asia, my Alaska contact readily accepted the reason given. He was a little surprised that I needed the information immediately. I was able to quiet any suspicions by appealing to his sophistication as an experienced high level staff officer who understood how illogical and unreasonable the demands of general officers could be. I also let him understand that General Johnson probably was under the gun to give a fast answer to Mr. McNamara or some Senator or maybe even the White House. I got my information in record breaking time via a second "scrambler" phone conversation.

The news was good, at least from our point of view. The battalions could be brought up to strength by using people already in Alaska except for about 40 who would have to be found elsewhere. That would be no problem. We would have our pick of 2000, most of whom would be sitting in Hawaii awaiting the arrival of the battalions, if the Chief of Staff decided to send them.

He did. The ODCSOPS issued orders to the Commanding General, US Army, Alaska, to ship the two battalions promptly to Hawaii after filling them with personnel in Alaska except for the 40 vacancies that had been reported to me. The ODCSPER was directed to divert the 2000 fillers to other assignments. We went through the motions, but by the time the orders were issued most of them were already in Hawaii. Some of them undoubtedly went with the Division, the rest were assigned to units in Hawaii and probably quickly requested the Army to bring their families to share their good fortune.

As one can imagine, the Commanding General in Alaska was not happy about losing his two infantry battalions. At his request we redesignated the battalions before their departure rather than upon their arrival in Honolulu as planned. In this way, the two original battalions remained on the books of the Alaskan command, even though at zero strength, awaiting the day when we could once again put officers and men into them. It was a long wait, although we sent a cable to the Commanding General promising to reconstitute his battalions as soon as possible.

As I recall it, the Division did not proceed to Vietnam any earlier than originally scheduled. After the Alaska battalions had arrived in Hawaii the Division Commanding General decided that their personnel needed to spend some extra time on Oahu in order to acclimate themselves to the climatic conditions of South Vietnam, so drastically different from those of Alaska.

Some months after the battalions had departed, I had another occasion to call Headquarters, U.S. Army, Alaska, via "scrambler" phone in order to obtain some classified data for some routine report or memorandum I was preparing. While I was waiting for my Alaska contact to reply, an agitated lieutenant colonel, Assistant to Lieutenant General Woolnough, the DCSPER, burst into my office to ask why I was asking for information from Alaska. I told him. I also expressed my surprise that such a routine request had aroused obvious front office concern. Before dashing back to General Woolnough he explained that the DCSPER had just received a call from the commanding general in Alaska wanting anxiously to know why Lieutenant Colonel Landis had called, stating that the last time Landis had called he had lost two battalions. He did not want the Pentagon playing any more games behind his back. Apparently General Woolnough's explanation and assurances calmed the Commanding General, because I shortly thereafter got my information.

Chapter 15

The Drawdown

SINCE the end of World War II the United States Army, Europe had consistently received from the Department of Defense and the Department of the Army the highest priority for support, except perhaps during the initial period of the Korean War, and even then care was taken not to diminish its strength. As a first lieutenant in 1950 serving in Germany I had my return to the United States postponed arbitrarily for six months, as did every other soldier in USAREUR, because replacements were not immediately available.

For the Korean War, however, the call-up of the Reserves and of the National Guard provided the initial buildup of strength that enabled the government to support a war in the Pacific while not bleeding the strength of its forces elsewhere. In fact, because of the apprehension created by the war that the USSR might be tempted to initiate an aggression in Europe, the strength of USAREUR's forces was not only maintained but augmented by National Guard and Reserve units.

For the war in Vietnam we did not have, by Presidential decision, the Reserves and National Guard to augment the peacetime army, a large part of which was in Europe. Initially, we could not use USAREUR as a part of our reservoir of trained personnel for assignment to deploying units. We did not, however, try to stabilize its strength as had been done during the Korean War. Soldiers continued to return to the United States as their normal overseas tours of duty ended. They became quickly available for assignment to units scheduled to go to Vietnam. At first we tried not to send anyone to Vietnam with less than twelve months in the United States since his last return from overseas. We soon had to make exceptions to this rule for certain skills for which the demand in Vietnam exceeded the supply. The number of exceptions grew regularly.

One of the earliest, if not the earliest, and certainly the longest lasting, of these was for helicopter pilots. The demand for them exceeded the supply from the beginning of the buildup and continued for years afterward. The causes were simple and immutable. General Westmoreland continually increased his requirements for helicopter units. It took about a year to train a helicopter pilot. The number of pilots we could train at any one time was set by the capacity of our training facilities. This capacity was a function of the availability of equipment, facilities, and instructors. It takes an appreciable time to increase the availability of each of these constraining factors.

In addition, for equipment and pilot instructors there were conflicting demands. We needed them to train new pilots. General Westmoreland needed them to fight a war.

In order to meet his demand while trying to build up the supply, we had to curtail the length of time helicopter pilots spent outside of Vietnam. It was not long before they were lucky if they could enjoy several months in the United States before being sent back to Vietnam or being assigned to a unit readying for deployment. Only those assigned to train pilots, assigned to other overseas commands, assigned to fly the President's helicopter, and other such high priority tasks, could count on longer times outside of Vietnam. Although helicopter pilots were the extreme case of insufficient numbers, there were other skills in a similar situation.

We were not authorized to pull people out of USAREUR to meet our needs in Vietnam. We could, however, change our policies toward people coming back from a tour in Europe. In the past a soldier having spent three years in Europe with his family could count on a protracted stay in the United States before being reassigned overseas. We decided that family life in Europe should be considered equivalent to family life in the United States. Consequently, a soldier returning from Europe was immediately eligible for reassignment to Vietnam. We could also choose not to replace all those returning. This we also did. When Headquarters, USAREUR, perceived what we were doing it launched a vociferous effort at the highest levels in the Department of Defense and the Department of the Army to have its traditional status as the bulwark of the free world's defense respected. The effort was preordained to failure.

In the spring of 1966 the Department of Defense approved a request from General Westmoreland for a massive buildup to be accomplished that year. Almost all of the requested units did not then exist. They would have to be created, manned, equipped, and trained. In order to meet the demand, and there was never any question about its being met 100%, the United States Army as a whole, less that part of it already in Vietnam, was going to have to be transformed into a manpower pool for Vietnam. We weren't sure that even then we could meet the requirements. The accuracy of the records of our personnel resources was not high enough to give us that assurance. We were virtually sure that we could not, in any case, meet the requirements with regard to the ranks and skill levels required. We had already adopted in the face of our dwindling pool of trained manpower the practice of deviating downward from the specified rank and skill level in order to fill vacancies in deploying units. If, for example, there was a position for a Corporal we would fill it with a Private First Class, if necessary; if there was a position for a Sergeant we would fill it with a Corporal. For units outside of Vietnam we did not long try to adhere to this policy. For them we often had to deviate two grades and skill levels when filling vacancies. For example, a Private First Class to take a Sergeant's place; a Private, even a very new Private, fresh from basic training, to fill a Corporal's shoes. As the buildup continued Bill Duba and I sometimes found it necessary to accept even a two-level deviation in order to get certain skills into deploying units.

Over time, of course, the situation ameliorated. The soldier who went to Vietnam a Private came back a Corporal, and if he stayed in the Army, he probably went back to Vietnam and returned a Staff Sergeant with a lot of experience behind those stripes.

We knew the problem would eventually disappear to the extent we could get people to re-enlist. And also to the extent that we could keep track of them.

As we progressed through the second year of the buildup we encountered an additional personnel problem. (I once crossed the path of a Major General, Division Commander, who had decreed that no such concept as "problem" existed. In the world of his division, there were only challenges and opportunities. He even forbid the use of the word "problem" by the personnel of his division. I never could decide whether "facing a problem" was a less affirmative act than "meeting a challenge" or "taking advantage of an opportunity.") The war in Vietnam required many skills that were either not needed at all elsewhere in the Army or were needed in far fewer numbers. Skills, such as, well digger, diver, mortuary specialist, locomotive engineer, stevedore, etc. When soldiers with these skills returned to the United States they were routinely assigned to positions in other skills. Either in a military specialty they had prior to being trained in the new skill for Vietnam or in a specialty for which they had to be retrained but for which there was a need in the Army outside of Vietnam.

The Stateside Army had no requirements for well diggers. When a well digger finished his tour in Vietnam there was nowhere to send him as a well digger. He would simply be assigned to fill whatever position needed to be filled. If he had had military experience before becoming a well digger, the personnel assignment agencies would make an effort to put him in a position requiring his previously acquired skill. If he had gone straight from basic training to well digging he would simply be assigned to fill the most urgent need. My colleagues who were responsible for ensuring that the Army had the correct number of people to do all the jobs to be done recognized fairly early that continuing these procedures would create two serious problems.

First, we would very probably lose track of our well digger. He would be in a rifle company somewhere as a Corporal, Section Leader. He would be identified on the Enhanced Enlisted Master Tape Record (EEMTR) with a Primary Military Occupational Specialty (PMOS) as an Infantry Unit Commander. The EEMTR would also show a secondary specialty, which could be that of well digger. It could also be that of another specialty in which the soldier had developed a skill either by experience or by training. A soldier could request what secondary specialty was shown on the EEMTR. The personnel people could insert a specialty they considered appropriate. Since well digger was an exotic and rare specialty with no requirements outside of Vietnam, it tended to be dropped from a soldier's record in favor of more widely needed specialties. So, the trained and experienced well digger disappeared from view.

The second and more serious effect was that we would always be sending inexperienced well diggers to Vietnam. The experienced ones who should have been available to teach and to return to Vietnam to command detachments had disappeared. In order to avoid these problems my colleagues created the Continental-United-States Sustaining Increment (CSI). The Pentagon authorized certain types of units in the United States to have 10% more people than their normally authorized number. This 10% increment was to be filled with soldiers returning from Vietnam with specified MOS. The selected MOS were those needed in Vietnam but not found elsewhere in the Army, or if found, were not needed in the same quantities. My colleagues did their best to select units to receive CSI positions that had some relationship to the skills we were trying to preserve. Well diggers could, for example, be assigned to water purification units of the Corps of Engineers. For other specialties, the relationship could be much more tenuous. The Army outside of Vietnam had no port operations whatsoever. So, stevedores would be assigned to almost any kind of unit at Fort Storey, Virginia, the home of the Transportation School, where whatever training or activities involving loading and unloading cargo were taking place. In any case, the one immutable criterion was that no one was authorized to change the PMOS that the soldier brought out of Vietnam. Like the USAREUR drawdown, the CSI was another step in converting the Army worldwide into a manpower pool for Vietnam.

In the spring of 1966, in order to meet the request of General Westmoreland for massive reinforcements, we requested the authority to take people out of Europe to meet the requirements of the units we programmed to activate in June. We told the decision makers that we had no other choices for finding the trained and experienced officers and non-commissioned officers needed to be the cadres for these units. We told them that the combat readiness of the United States Army in Europe would suffer. We promised to replace without undue delay every man withdrawn, but we also told them we would be sending Privates and Second Lieutenants fresh from training to replace experienced Sergeants and Captains. We told them we had no idea when we would have available the Sergeants and Captains to bring USAREUR back to its traditional readiness posture. The decision makers really had no decision to make. There were no choices to select from.

As soon as formal approval was given, the Office of Personnel Operations furnished to Headquarters, USAREUR, a list of the number and types of people needed. With its usual flair for taking the easy way out, OPO transmitted the entire list of requirements without screening it to pull out those specialties that were not to be found in USAREUR, such as, stevedores, well diggers, divers, etc. It was not until after the Personnel On Station Date for the first units scheduled to deploy had come and gone that I discovered what OPO had neglected to report it had done. As a result, we had to do our usual scurrying around to make last minute assignments for a lot more people than we anticipated.

For reasons I no longer remember, we activated almost all of the units requested by General Westmoreland for 1966 in the month of June, and on two specific dates. As I recall, they were the 20th and 30th. In the weeks and months preceding these dates, tens of thousands of people had begun moving from their old units in Europe and the United States to relocate their families and to visit parents, sweethearts, and friends. Then, in the days before the 20th and the 30th, another movement of these same thousands, less wives and children, took place as they homed in on their new units.

Our decision to start everything on two dates only ten days apart created havoc. We placed a tremendous load on the Army's capability to transport people and their possessions. We forced posts and garrisons to handle hordes of incoming soldiers in a short span of time. I don't know why we hadn't thought of these consequences. Some one of us experienced staff officers should have. Working within the walls of the Pentagon we simply failed to imagine the effect of our decision on the people who had to live it. Not only ourselves, but everyone involved, through intermediate headquarters down to the headquarters of the posts and garrisons, knew well ahead what was going to transpire. Nobody raised a voice to say: "Hey! Do you realize what you are doing? There must be a better way." I can only offer as explanation that one year after the initial deployment of combat units to Vietnam the Army from top to bottom, from Alaska to Europe, had been forced to recognize that support of the effort in Vietnam was its sole priority. People accepted making extraordinary efforts without question in the name of Vietnam. Even when those efforts were caused by ill conceived decisions.

Chapter 16

Unit Readiness

THE reader may remember that when I arrived in the Pentagon I was supposed to be one of a small group (2 other lieutenant colonels) responsible for monitoring the personnel aspects of the Army's Unit Readiness system. The reader will also recall, however, that my second day of duty saw me diverted to the role of the ODCPER representative on the newly established committee to oversee unit deployments to Vietnam. For my first year of Pentagon duty this was my Number One priority. Nonetheless, John Kiser ensured that I participate, at least part time, as a monitor of the unit readiness system. At the end of that year with the reassignment of Lieutenant Colonel Kiser I became the Chief of Readiness Branch. I dropped off the unit deployment committee and turned the job of ODCSPER representative over to Major Fred Miller, who had joined the Branch after the departure of Lieutenant Colonel Tallman. After John Kiser's departure, Lieutenant Colonel Charles Waters arrived to fill the third position in the Branch.

As a cadet at West Point and then as a young lieutenant I was quite unaware of any concept of unit readiness. I don't know when the United States Army decided that it needed a method of evaluating the combat readiness of its units in peacetime. I do feel that the Army had developed some sort of method to judge a combat unit's readiness to accomplish its mission, but I was not aware of it. I believe that during the war, units, such as newly created divisions, were put through a strenuous field exercise to determine that they were ready for deployment to a combat theater. These field exercises were directed primarily to test the ability of commanders from the squad leader to the division commander to function effectively under stressful conditions, which were meant to simulate actual combat less the death and destruction. The ability of the individual combat soldier to accomplish his mission was not particularly emphasized except his ability to go without sleep for days on end, to function without eating regularly, to function in all kinds of weather.

When I joined my first unit as a second lieutenant after the war readiness was not an issue. In 1947 the United States Constabulary had the mission of controlling the border between the United States Zone of Occupation in Germany and that of the Zone of Occupation of the Soviet Union, as well as the border between the United States Zone of Occupation in Germany and Czechoslovakia. In addition, Constabulary units had certain police functions in the interior of the United States Zone of Occupation, such as, raiding displaced persons camps in search of contraband, setting up speed traps on Autobahns, etc. The United States Constabulary was a police unit and was not concerned with combat readiness. Until the Berlin Blockade. As of January 1, 1949, my Constabulary squadron (the equivalent of a battalion) ceased all police operations. The unit was redesignated the 3rd Reconnaissance Battalion of the 14th Armored Cavalry Regiment. Instead of armored cars we were equipped with tanks, light tanks in the reconnaissance companies, medium tanks in the tank company. Instead of being concerned about illegal border crossers, we began to train intensively to accomplish a combat mission.

In the spring of 1949 my Reconnaissance Battalion participated in the first Zone-wide maneuver since the end of the war that involved all the U.S. Army troops in Germany. This training exercise simulated an actual combat situation less the death and destruction. This Zone-wide maneuver was repeated in the fall of 1949 and in the Spring and Fall of 1950, but with different scenarios. I assume this type of Zone-wide maneuver continued until the Occupation was ended. I can't imagine that U.S. Army units were permitted any longer to roam up and down the highways, to set up defensive positions in the middle of towns, to run across farmers' fields (This was discouraged, but was done if the pseudo-tactical situation required it. Reimbursement for damages was made.). After the end of the Occupation maneuvers and field exercises were limited to military training areas, such as, Grafenwöhr, Wildflecken, Munsingen, etc.

I don't know when the United States Army decided that it needed a system for evaluating the combat readiness of its units in peacetime. I do know that various methods for testing and judging the combat readiness of a unit, the elements of an embryonic system, existed when I was a young officer in Occupied Germany. At that time a few years after the end of World War II one of the elements of this not-yet system was the Annual Training Test (ATT). This was a field exercise, normally of 3 days duration, in which a unit was placed in a simulated combat situation and was given a series of missions to accomplish. For a combat unit these were usually occupation of an assembly area, a night march to an attack position, an attack, a withdrawal, the establishment of a defensive position. Normally, the unit subjected to such an annual test was a battalion. Smaller units, such as, companies and platoons, and larger units, such as, regiments, brigades, divisions, did not undergo them. The battalion would receive a grade, usually either Satisfactory or Unsatisfactory. Woe to the battalion that failed the test. It usually meant an extended period of field training with a second test and oftentimes, the replacement of the battalion commander.

The ATT had the drawback of being conducted only once a year. A unit could be qualified as "Satisfactory" in June and be an entirely different unit 4 months later, with personnel turnover, equipment shortages, inadequate training, etc. In addition, the test did not take into consideration equipment shortages in assessing a unit's capability to accomplish its mission. If a unit accomplished satisfactorily each of the combat missions assigned within the scope of the test, it didn't make any difference whether the unit had 100%, 80%, 60%, etc. of its materiel and equipment operational. For example, if a tank company with 3 tank platoons, each platoon authorized 5 tanks, had only 10 of its 15 tanks, if the mission, let us say, an attack, was properly conducted, the unit would receive a "Satisfactory" rating, even though it would have been probably incapable of accomplishing its full mission as specified in its Table of Organization and Equipment

Whether the ATT existed prior to World War II, I do not know. I do not know whether the United States Army had any system whatsoever for evaluating the combat readiness of its units prior to World War II. I do not know when the ATT was developed and implemented. I first encountered it in the summer of 1950. Prior to that time the Constabulary Squadrons did not undergo Annual Training Tests. Was it because these tests had not yet been adopted by the Army or was it because of the special missions of the United States Constabulary? It was in June of 1950 that my battalion, the 3rd Battalion of the 14th Armored Cavalry Regiment underwent its first ATT. And it was also my first.

I encountered another element in testing and judging the combat readiness of a unit in 1949. This was a test instituted by Major General I. D. White when he took over the United States Constabulary in 1948 and after the conversion of its Constabulary Regiments into Armored Cavalry Regiments. He established a Combat Readiness Competition at the platoon level. The competition was in the form of the Annual Training Test I have described above, but with gunnery exercises added for the tanks and mortars. First, each battalion selected its best platoons, usually by competitive exercises similar to ATT's. Second, there were competitions within each regiment to select the best platoons in the regiment in each category, i.e., tank platoon, reconnaissance platoon, rifle platoon, mortar platoon. (General White had decided to modify the organization of the Reconnaissance Battalions as prescribed by the Department of the Army. In the Constabulary, a Reconnaissance Company did not consist of three Reconnaissance Platoons, each with a Tank Section, a Scout Section, a Rifle Squad, and a Mortar Squad, but of only two Reconnaissance Platoons, each containing only a Tank Section and a Scout Section. The Rifle Squads were grouped into a Rifle Platoon. The Mortar Squads of each of the Reconnaissance Companies were transferred to the Battalion's Headquarters and Headquarters Company, where they were formed into a Mortar Platoon.) Then, there were competitions at the brigade level to select the best platoons in each brigade. And, finally, there was a competition between the best platoons in each brigade (There were only two brigades in the U.S. Constabulary.) to select the best platoon in each category among all the platoons in the United States Constabulary. The first competitions took place in 1949. One of my reconnaissance platoons (I was a company commander in 1949-50.) won the Constabulary competition in 1950. I do not know how long these competitions continued. The United States Constabulary was deactivated in 1952.

Another aspect of the not-yet-system to evaluate the combat readiness of U.S. Army units was in the form of a written report prepared by a battalion commander presenting his judgment on the ability of his unit to accomplish its mission. Every combat unit is organized according to a Table of Organization and Equipment (TOE) or a Modified TOE. These documents not only prescribe the personnel and equipment that are authorized for the unit, but also specify what missions can be accomplished by the unit when fully equipped, manned, and trained. Given the mind set inculcated in the U.S. Army officer corps and the American military mythology of winning against overwhelming enemy superiority, battalion commanders did not accept the idea that a unit with less than its allotment of equipment and qualified personnel could not accomplish the missions prescribed for their units. To have so stated in an official report would, in their minds, have been an admission of incompetence. Consequently, these commander readiness evaluations were more often than not totally unrealistic. In fact, they acquired the sobriquet of the "can do" report, because the commanders invariably declared in some form or another, "Despite shortages of equipment and personnel the battalion can do whatever it is ordered to do."

I don't know when these reports became required. I don't recall their existence during my years of troop duty in Germany. I first encountered them when I joined the Third Armored Cavalry Regiment in June 1960. I don't remember the frequency at which they were required to be made. Their preparation was still required when I left the Regiment in October 1962.

Another aspect of this embryonic system was the unscheduled monthly alert exercise. This was put into effect in the United States Army in Europe either late 1950 or early 1951. Once a month, at an unscheduled and therefore unknown time, Headquarters, USAREUR, would notify all USAREUR units of an alert. The requirement was that a unit be clear of its barracks area en route to a predesignated, prereconnoitered assembly area with all its materiel and equipment, to include ammunition for all weapons, in less than 45 minutes, ready to engage in combat. Obviously, this required considerable prior planning and preparation. Ammunition had to be stowed ahead of time on combat vehicles or loaded on trucks. Soldiers had to have packs with essential clothing and toiletries ready at all times. Vehicles had to be fueled. The concept was, "Take everything you need to engage in protracted combat, as though you were never returning to these barracks." These alerts were practiced in Europe for many years, certainly, at least, until the dissolution of the Soviet Union. In 1967, when I commanded an Armored Cavalry Squadron in South Korea, we also had quarterly unscheduled alert exercises.

Still another aspect of this amorphous unit readiness system was the annual inspection of battalion-sized units plus regimental and division headquarters by the Office of the Inspector General. These inspections probably predated any concept of unit readiness, but in view of their comprehensiveness they could be deemed a part of such a system in that they looked at all aspects of a unit's condition except, its capability to perform tactical missions. They considered and graded the maintenance of a unit's equipment, the adequacy of its training, the condition of its materiel and equipment, the efficacy of its administration, etc.

Another means of judging a unit was the Command Maintenance Management Inspection (CMMI). This was also an annual inspection conducted by higher headquarters on its subordinate units. It concentrated exclusively on the effectiveness of a unit in maintaining its materiel and equipment. The AR defines it as follows: "This inspection provides an indication of the status of unit materiel readiness and effectiveness of the overall maintenance program to include shop operations, tools and test equipment, personnel, training, records and reports, repair parts supply, publications, and facilities."

I would like to think that someday some military historian will take an interest in the history of the efforts of the United States Army to evaluate the readiness of its units with respect to their capability of accomplishing their assigned combat missions. This historian could even look at other armies to see how they evaluated their units. Both past and present. Did the United States Army make any effort to evaluate the combat readiness of its units in World War II, in World War I and in the Civil War? Did Napoleon do it? Did Frederick the Great do it? Do the British, French, German, Russian, and Chinese Armies do it today? What about the German Army in World War II?

In any case, when I went into the Readiness Branch of the Office of the Deputy Chief of Staff for Personnel all the disparate elements I have mentioned--field exercises, maneuvers, combat leadership competitions, annual inspections by the Inspector General, alert exercises, annual training tests, "can do" reports, command maintenance management inspections—had been assembled into a single comprehensive, integrated concept of Unit Readiness. This concept was codified by Army Regulation (AR) 220-1. The version in effect in September 1965 was dated July 1965. There was undoubtedly an earlier version and maybe more than one earlier version. My guess is, however, that the first version would not predate 1962. I have no recollection whatsoever of having filled out the quarterly readiness reports required by the Army Regulation during my service with the 3rd Armored Cavalry Regiment (July 1960–September 1962).

During my second year in the Pentagon I was involved in updating the readiness regulation. I was responsible for the personnel aspects in it. A revised version was published in February 1967. How many versions succeeded that one, I do not know. Whether the concept of Unit Readiness still exists in the Army I do not know

As stated in the first paragraph of the 1967 version of the Regulation, "This regulation establishes uniform readiness standards and reporting procedures which are designed to assist headquarters, Department of the Army (DA) and commanders at all levels in making the most effective use of available resources and in determining requirements for additional resources."

The objectives of this readiness system were set forth in paragraph 5 of the Regulation: "The primary objectives of the Army readiness system are to insure that each unit has its authorized personnel with the required skills available for duty; that its authorized equipment is on hand and maintained in an operational condition; that its needed supplies are on hand; and that each unit is maintaining a state of training which will permit accomplishment of the mission reflected in the authorization document under which it is organized. Effectively utilized and supervised, the system will permit Department of the Army to accomplish the following:

a. Provide a basis for orderly distribution of actual and programmed resources.
b. Provide justification for requesting additional programmed resources from the Department of Defense.
c. Determine Army-wide and command-wide readiness trends.
d. Identify readiness problems which require resolution."

The guiding principle of the system established by AR 220-1 was 100% objectivity in reporting. The criteria were either quantitative or required a "yes" or "no" answer. The AR tried to reduce to an absolute minimum all subjective evaluations. Paragraph 9d of the AR stated, "It is important that unit readiness reports reflect the true condition of a unit...if the unit commander has complied with regulations and has exhausted the resources at his disposal and the objective factors on which the readiness report is based indicate that his unit readiness condition (REDCON) is below its assigned readiness capability (REDCAPE), no higher commander in the chain of command will consider this fact as reflecting unfavorably upon the unit commander."

To judge the level of readiness of a unit two readiness categories were established as standards. The first was the Readiness

Requirement, known as REDCAT. The acronym REDCAT came from Readiness Category, even though the AR uses the term "requirement." "REDCAT for individual units represent the total requirements for personnel and equipment for best accomplishment of assigned missions. REDCAT are derived from general war and contingency plans, including the deployment schedules associated with those plans; from the vulnerability of units to attack by potential enemies..." Three levels of REDCAT were established: Level 1, known as "C1," required 100% of prescribed level of equipment and personnel and specified that the unit was "Ready to execute any TOE/MTOE...mission within 24 hours for a sustained period." ."..any TOE/MTOE mission" simply meant any mission which the unit was designed to perform at 100% strength. Level 2, i.e., C2, was based on less than 100% of full personnel and equipment and prescribed that the unit was "Ready to execute any TOE/MTOE mission if allowed 15 days to fill resource shortages," and "can execute TOE/MTOE mission but not for a sustained period." C3 meant a still lesser percentage of full TOE/MTOE personnel and equipment and prescribed that the unit was "Ready to execute any TOE/MTOE mission if allowed 30 days to fill resource shortages and/or complete training, but "can partially execute TOE/MTOE mission for a limited period."

For example, in 1965 an infantry division in Western Germany faced by Soviet armed forces would be designated a REDCAT C1 unit. An airborne division based in the United States and part of the strategic reserve would also be designated a REDCAT C1 unit. An infantry division based in the United States and not scheduled for immediate deployment in case of an emergency could be designated either a REDCAT C2 or C3 unit depending upon its planned deployment schedule.

The second standard was designated the Readiness Capability or REDCAPE. This standard reflected the difference between the requirements in personnel and equipment reflected by a unit's wartime mission, i.e., its REDCAT, and what the Army could actually support with authorized personnel and equipment levels. The AR stated, "In order to retain the true requirements

(REDCAT) as an objective, while at the same time conducting the day-to-day business with the resources made available to the Army by higher authority, a level of readiness is established which is within the capability of the Army to support with programmed personnel spaces...and equipment---this is the unit REDCAPE."

The levels for a unit's REDCAPE were identical to those for the unit's REDCAT.

For example, that REDCAT C1 infantry division in Europe may have a REDCAPE of C2, because its authorized composition lacked one of its battalions because of a lack of personnel and equipment resources allocated to its higher command by the Department of the Army, which was constrained by insufficient resources authorized by the Congress.

Every calendar quarter all combat units were required to submit a report on their actual level of readiness. This Readiness Condition, or REDCON, was determined by the unit commander based on his knowledge of conditions within the unit. The AR stated, "In order that REDCON be measured objectively and uniformly, common factors in the areas of personnel, training, and logistics have been selected as readiness indicators." The designated readiness indicators were (1) Personnel (Operating Strength, Military Occupational Specialty, i.e., per cent of "personnel in operating strength who are qualified to perform the duties of the position to which assigned."), (2) Training (Refresher Training, i.e., "Mandatory subjects, arms qualification and physical fitness"), Squad/Crew Proficiency, Unit Proficiency, Field Exercises, Mission Training), and (3) Logistics (Equipment on Hand, Unit Equipment Serviceability, Unit Equipment Deployability, Unit Loads, i.e. prescribed amounts of ammunition, gasoline/diesel, and rations to be carried by the unit, Command Maintenance Management Inspection)

There were four levels of readiness condition defined as follows: "a. REDCON C1. Unit is fully capable of performing the full TOE mission for which organized or designed. b. REDCON C2. Unit is capable of performing the full TOE mission for which organized or designed, but has minor deficiencies which reduce its ability to conduct sustained operations. C. REDCON C3 Unit has deficiencies of such magnitude as to limit its capability to perform the full TOE mission for which organized or designed, but is capable nonetheless of conducting operations for a limited period. D. REDCON C4. Unit has deficiencies of such magnitude as to limit severely its capability to perform the full TOE mission for which organized or designed."

In order for the unit commander to determine the REDCON of his unit objective factors were established for all of the readiness indicators listed above. For example, for the Personnel Strength indicator a REDCON C1 rating meant that" Operating strength [was] not less than 95% [of] 'full TOE' [strength]," C2, not less than 85%, C3, not less than 75%, C4, less than 75%. For the Training Unit Proficiency indicator a REDCON C1 meant that, "100% of all platoons and companies specified by full TOE have satisfactorily accomplished ATT (Annual Training Test)...," C2, 80-99%, C3, 60-79%, C4, less than 60%. For the Logistics Equipment on Hand indicator a REDCON C1 meant that 90% of all the materiel designated in the full TOE was at least 90% on hand, C2, at least 80% was on hand of 90% of each item of materiel specified in the full TOE, C3, at least 70%, C4, 70% was on hand of less than 90% of the full TOE authorization. For example, let's take a tank company authorized under its full TOE to have 17 tanks, 3 5-tank platoons and 2 tanks in the company headquarters. Ninety per cent of 17 is 15.3, or 15 tanks. For a C1 rating 90% of those 15 tanks must be on hand, i.e., 13.8 or 14 tanks. Let's say, because of shortages of the tanks specified by the TOE, higher headquarters cannot support a full TOE for this tank company. So, under an MTOE the company has 3 platoons of 4 tanks each and only one tank in company headquarters, i.e., 4 tanks less than full TOE, or 13 tanks. Therefore, this company can have only a C2 rating for this particular item. The Equipment on Hand rating for the whole company is the aggregate of the REDCON ratings for all items of materiel and equipment authorized by the full TOE.

The readiness system spelled out by the regulation was well designed to meet its objective, ."..to assist Headquarters, Department of the Army...and commanders at all levels in making the most effective use of available resources and in determining requirements for additional resources." Unfortunately, it was never as successful as it should have been. The major factor in its lack of success was that commanders looked upon the quarterly reports as an attempt by Department of the Army to grade them on their management of their units, whether these were battalions, regiments, divisions, etc. This was an attitude shared by all levels of command from captains to generals. This was an attitude that persisted even though Department of the Army through visits by its Readiness Teams attempted regularly and frequently to make commanders understand that it was not a report card. Commanders at all levels looked upon it as a comment on their competence, particularly when the reported REDCON was less than the designated REDCAPE. The drawdown in Europe in 1966 is a striking example of how this attitude permeated even the highest levels of command.

One of the inevitable effects of the drawdown should have been a decrease in the readiness of the Army in Europe to perform its combat mission. It was not possible to pull tens of thousands of qualified, experienced soldiers out of a command, replace them with recruits fresh out of basic training and second lieutenants fresh out of OCS without causing a deterioration in the command's combat readiness. In the Army General Staff we believed that the REDCON of the units in Europe would plummet for several reporting periods and only slowly get back to a satisfactory level. In fact, in preparing the message to announce the drawdown, we wanted Headquarters, USAREUR, to know that we in the Pentagon were cognizant of what was going to happen. We didn't want them to come back at us in the succeeding months with complaints that the shortages were opening doors into Western Europe for the armed might of the USSR, this being their hallowed ploy to get what they wanted. We put a sentence into the message telling Headquarters, USAREUR, we knew their units' readiness would suffer and that we could not forecast when we could make them whole again. We also included the sentence in order to keep the upper reaches of the Department of Defense off our backs in the following months. We wanted the record to show that those who had ordered the drawdown knew ahead of time the consequences of their act.

We waited anxiously the first quarterly readiness reports after the drawdown. When they arrived we discovered to our amazement and chagrin that the REDCONs as reported for the major units in Europe had not fallen at all. On the other hand, the news was happily received at higher levels. There would be no need to explain to Congress any falling off of our European readiness. No one was interested in trying to determine how the apparent miracle had occurred.

One of the great obstacles in the Army's attempt to create a system that would accurately and objectively measure unit readiness for combat was the attitude of commanders at all levels. The attitude that nothing is impossible—"The difficult we do immediately; the impossible may take a little longer"-- or, at the least, that duty requires that the impossible be attempted and that to admit that something cannot be done is shameful, was instilled in plebes at West Point and passed by generations of graduates to the officer corps of the Army. Commanders considered it an uncomplimentary reflection upon their competence to have to declare that their units could not perform their missions. Even when such a condition was the result of shortages of people and equipment created by inadequate support from higher echelons, shortages over which they had no control and which they could not remedy.

Why didn't the unit REDCONS in the U.S. Army in Europe decline? Simply because the commanders made a judgment that the privates and second lieutenants who replaced the sergeants and captains who had departed were as fully capable as their predecessors after 2-3 months on the job without any specialized training for the positions they occupied. The commanders stormed through a loophole granted them by the AR, namely, ."..personnel...who are performing duties or being trained to perform duties to meet the [skills} requirement of the unit will be considered qualified when in the judgment of the unit commander the individual can perform the required duties."

From my personal experience on a smaller scale I knew full well that 3 months were insufficient to turn a private fresh out of Basic Training into a qualified Squad Leader or Tank Crew Commander. In the Fall of 1948 the enlistments of many of the Corporals and Sergeants of my Squadron expired. These were soldiers who had re-enlisted shortly after the end of the war in order to enjoy life in Occupied Germany. Now they were ready to go home. My Squadron received the bulk of their replacements just at the time we were changing from a Constabulary Squadron to an Armored Cavalry Reconnaissance Battalion. These replacements arrived when we were receiving our new equipment and undergoing training at the Grafenwöhr Training Area. I was selected to return to our home station to receive the replacements for our Troop and to give them a sort of indoctrination training on service in Germany and in the Squadron's standards of conduct and discipline. When the remnants of the Squadron (As I recall, we had lost almost half the enlisted personnel in the Troop.) returned to the home station with the new equipment, the recruits were assigned to fill empty positions. We had to name some of these recruits Acting Corporals and Acting Sergeants. Selecting which ones to designate was difficult, since we had only meager knowledge of their capabilities. We were forced to decide by considering such superficial characteristics as demeanor, apparent attitude, conduct, etc. We made a lot of wrong choices. Then we had to teach them how to use the equipment. We had to teach the Acting Corporals and Sergeants how to be leaders. For months the Troops of the Squadron were not as effective as they should have been, were not as effective as they would have been without the loss of experienced personnel.

The same situation must have prevailed in many units in Germany after the drawdown. Yet the reporting did not reflect this. The ingrained attitude of the U.S. Army officer and his reluctance to submit a report that he thought could reflect on his competence combined to falsify the true state of the United States Army in Europe.

Another example of the defeat of the objective of the unit readiness system comes from my experience in Korea. I left the

Pentagon in the summer of 1967 to take over the command of the 2d Squadron of the 10th Armored Cavalry Regiment, which was a part of the 7th Infantry Division. This Squadron was operating under a Modified TOE that eliminated the authorized Air Cavalry Troop. As a result, the REDCON for the Squadron could never be higher than C4, regardless of any efforts made by me or my staff and subordinate commanders. In order to prepare for the quarterly submission of the Unit Readiness Report the Division Commander required that each subordinate battalion-sized unit submit a "practice report" at the end of the second month of the quarter. The division then examined these reports to see what it could do to improve the REDCON of any units that were less than their REDCAPES.

The Tank battalion of the Division had a REDCAPE 1 assigned to it. If its "practice report" showed a REDCON 2 or even 3, the Division required that actions be taken to raise that to a REDCON 1 in the month ahead. Invariably, these actions were to the detriment of my Squadron, since it could never be anything but a REDCON 4 unit and since it was the only divisional unit with comparable equipment. With respect to personnel, this was accomplished by diverting replacements arriving during the month for my Squadron to the Tank Battalion, since only my Squadron had Military Occupational Specialties similar to those in the Tank battalion. With respect to equipment, either spare parts that my Squadron had requisitioned were diverted to the Tank Battalion so that its vehicles would be operational or in extremis I was required to "cannibalize" my vehicles to provide parts for those of the Tank Battalion. John Kiser, who was commanding an infantry battalion in the division, and I both complained to the Division G-3 about this practice as subverting the intention of the Regulation, but to no avail.

A final word on unit readiness: the United States Army outside of Vietnam by the end of 1966 was in dire straits. It could not have punched its way out of a paper bag. In the continental United States only the 82nd Airborne Division was fully operational, although suffering from the turnover of their personnel to support the effort in Vietnam. The 101st Airborne Division lacked one of its brigades, already in Vietnam (The rest of the Division would deploy to that country in 1967.). The two armored divisions at Fort Hood and the 5th Mechanized Infantry Division at Camp Carson were essentially transformed into Replacement Training Centers to handle the influx of draftees that could not be handled by the designated Replacement Training Centers. The 11th Armored Cavalry Regiment was preparing to deploy to Vietnam. The situation of the United States Army in Europe I have described above. It continued to be the primary source of experienced replacements for Vietnam, as returnees from that country were assigned there only to be shipped off again after about a year (It was even shorter for helicopter pilots, who were lucky to have several months between tours.).

Chapter 17

DA Versus DOD

CONGRESS was quite sensitive to the effect the burgeoning Vietnam War was having on our capability to face the Soviet ground threat in Europe. Mr. McNamara frequently had to explain before Congressional committees his regularly stated position that our capability had not suffered despite the buildup in Vietnam. For one of these appearances, the Office of the Joint Chief Chiefs of Staff had prepared a schedule for a European buildup to face a hypothetical threat of Russian aggression. It assumed the mobilization of the Reserves and the National Guard. It showed the times in weeks necessary to put major combat units (divisions, separate brigades and regiments) into Europe. None of the times was realistic. They approached the fantastic. They would have had to be doubled, even tripled and quadrupled, to have achieved at least a modicum of plausibility.

My office was the point of contact for the action officer on the Joint Chiefs of Staff to get a chop on the proposed time tables. On my recommendation, General Izenour refused to chop. Negotiations began. We rewrote the schedule, proposing what we considered to be reasonable time delays. The Joint Staff would not accept them, not because they didn't agree with the figures, but because they couldn't possibly show such figures to Congress. We haggled. There were proposals and counterproposals. We finally achieved an agreement in which both sides won. The figures remained essentially as they were initially proposed by the Joint Staff, but they were extensively footnoted. The footnotes described the assumptions on which the figures were based. For example, one footnote made the assumption that the personnel of the mobilized units would report to their assigned stations within seven days after mobilization was proclaimed. Even in the dark days of December 1941, when there was a general apprehension that Japan was going to invade the

United States, the mobilized reservists and the National Guard members were given a month to put their affairs in order and report to their duty stations. Another footnote assumed there was sufficient rail transportation conveniently located at all the posts and camps to move the units without delay to the nearest ports. Another footnote assumed that there would be sufficient air and sea transportation waiting at these ports to move the units to Europe immediately. In reality, there were not enough trains, planes, or ships in the whole stock of transportation resources in the United States to lift the hundreds of thousands of troops with their equipment on the schedule indicated. And even if there had been enough, the decision to requisition and divert them from other uses would have meant a total cessation of civilian commercial transportation of all kinds, not to mention cessation of support of the forces in Vietnam. Moreover, the simple formality of requisitioning civilian transportation means setting up an organization to manage and control them, means taking the time needed for reconfiguring them to accommodate military loads. These time delays would have far exceeded the times proposed for moving all the units to Europe. The footnotes did not even try to assume that there were sufficient airports in the United States and Europe to handle the projected massive airlift on the proposed schedule. The problem was simply not even addressed. The footnote regarding sea transportation assumed, not only that there were sufficient vessels to move the equipment and supplies, but also that they were conveniently located at the appropriate ports ready to take on cargo. The ultimate footnote assumed that all the Reserve and National Guard units were fully equipped and trained. Like all the others, it did not come close to approximating the real world.

When all the footnotes were in place to explain the figures, we chopped. I do not know whether Mr. McNamara took the schedule to Capitol Hill. There were subsequent reports in the press that seemed to indicate that the time schedules had been presented to Congress. The press reports made no mention of assumptions. Did the press not understand their significance? Did the press never see the assumptions and, therefore, assume that the figures were based upon reality? Did Congress ever see the assumptions? One of my colleagues suggested that the assumptions were simply clipped off the bottom of the schedule before it was submitted to Congress. For those of us powerless to change the system it appeared to be another manifestation of the cynical maxim of the Pentagon staff officer that anything, however divorced from reality and reason, could be held out as fact as long as it was properly footnoted.

It was not unusual that assumptions on which decisions were based were, when convenient, simply forgotten. It was not unusual for the decision makers to act as though the assumptions had never been stated. When these conveniently forgotten assumptions dealt with consequences that would probably occur if the assumptions were not realistic, the decision makers would act as though the consequences were the result of causes other than their decisions. They, therefore, tended not to accept the consequences and expected us "Indians" to overcome them. Miracles were not in our bag of tricks. Sophistry was. With the detachable footnote and the specious assumption the Army was learning to use the gimmicks of the public relations and advertising trades. The trouble was that the Army was using them on itself as well as on the public.

Chapter 18

The Pacing Units

THE best and the worst of the Army's concentrated devotion to supporting the country's effort in Vietnam was epitomized by the "Pacing Units." Secretary of the Army Stanley Resor recognized that the massive buildup scheduled for 1966 created problems, not only for us the activators and dispatchers, but also for the Army in Vietnam, which would be receiving, integrating, and employing the units. The infrastructure, civilian and military, necessary to support combat units did not exist in Vietnam. We were creating the infrastructure at the same time we were sending the units. There were numerous instances where, because of a lack of specialized people and equipment and the length of time needed to develop well trained units, these infrastructure units were scheduled to arrive after the combat units they were supposed to support. One glaring example was the port terminal companies. These units were needed to offload incoming cargo and troop ships. Yet most of them were scheduled to arrive in country after the mass of the units and equipment to be offloaded. The same was true of the tugboat companies. The same was true of the Engineer construction battalions that were to build the camps to house the units and headquarters.

Secretary Resor sent a memorandum to the Army Staff departments in the spring of 1966 citing the need to have an adequate infrastructure in place before the arrival of the combat units. In order to achieve this, he designated certain units as being essential to being in country before the mass of combat units arrived. He named them "pacing units." Their presence in Vietnam would pace the deployment of the other units. His memorandum did not suggest delaying the deployment of combat units until the supporting "pacing" units could be put into place. He directed rather that the Army Staff use all its imagination, creativity, initiative, resourcefulness, etc., to expedite the dispatch of these units to Vietnam as early as possible and certainly before the deployment of the combat units. A laudable goal. Unfortunately, most of the Secretary's "pacing units" had deployment dates well after most of the combat units. And for very good reasons. We didn't have the people. We didn't have the equipment. The time needed to train these units to function properly generally exceeded the time to train combat units. The achievement of Mr. Resor's goal would require more than extraordinary staff work. It would need an event in the category of a miracle.

Nonetheless, he directed that Colonel Wagstaff report to him weekly in writing, "pacing unit" by "pacing unit," what the Army Staff was doing to hasten their dispatch. He specified that he expected to see the report each Tuesday. This was, as far as I was concerned, an unfortunate choice of a day. Wagstaff's people needed the information from the members of the Deployment Committee on Monday at the latest in order to prepare the consolidated and coordinated report. My boss, General Izenour, wanted to see what I intended to provide before I turned it over. This meant doing my work by Thursday or accepting to work over the weekend to make any changes he wanted.

The preparation of the first report did not go smoothly. Wagstaff's people exhorted us to come up with original, imaginative, innovative ideas for the first report. It was clear that Wagstaff wanted to impress the Secretary of the Army. Yet, I was not completely clear what the problems were going to be with the "Pacing Units," many of which hadn't yet even been activated. There were a dozen or more different kinds of units: port terminal companies, tugboat companies, railroad operating detachments, construction battalions, quartermaster companies, helicopter units, port operating companies, well digger detachments, etc. We knew that we would have problems with all of them in finding the right kinds of people and in getting them to their units on time. We handled this kind of problem every day. We thought we routinely handled them imaginatively, innovatively, creatively, as well as expeditiously. How in the hell was I supposed to come up with newly imaginative, creative, innovative, etc., ways to handle them? One of the first things I did was to ask Bill Duba's' successor (By this time Bill had happily departed to the Panama Canal Zone. I never did establish the same rapport with his successor that I had with him. Probably because he was more a liaison officer between the Major General, Chief, OPO, and me rather than like Bill, an operator who personally directed the assignment of individuals.) to get me a personnel status report on those units already activated and to let me know what had already been done to eliminate any reported shortages. I also asked him to give me a forecast as to what specialties were going to be the most difficult to provide. I didn't know what I was going to do with this information when I got it. I asked for it primarily to get my friends and colleagues working for Colonel Wagstaff off my back by giving them the impression of activity on my part.

It was not a happy week for me. It became clear as the days progressed toward Friday that I was not going to have anything to present to my boss before the weekend. Amidst the daily frenzy I had not found any time to essay my imagination, creativity, etc. I reluctantly had to inform General Izenour that I would not be able to work on the report until Saturday. Without fuss he offered to come in Sunday morning to look at my draft. This meant that not only would I have all day Saturday to prepare the draft but also most of Sunday to make any changes he wanted. I came into my office early Saturday morning ready and able to devote myself exclusively to Mr. Resor's "Pacing Units." Colonel Wagstaff's people were not particularly pleased to learn that they would have nothing from me before midday Monday. Anything I prepared over the weekend would have to be typed and approved by General Izenour before transmittal. Their last words of encouragement were "You'd better have something good!"

I worked all day Saturday, all Saturday evening, and most of Saturday night. I finally went home toward dawn, got a couple of hours sleep, bathed, shaved, dressed, breakfasted, and went back to the Pentagon to meet the general. The reason I worked so long was that newly creative, innovative, imaginative ideas were hard to conjure. I no longer remember what I actually proposed. I know that my effort to expedite the movement of units, most of which did not yet exist, and, therefore, the problems of which were only potential, led me to propose drastic changes in policies and procedures. I knew full well that by the time we could have had the changes approved the units concerned would be beyond needing their help. Yet I couldn't envision any other way of meeting Mr. Resor's directive. I wasn't pleased with my work. I dreaded having to show it to General Izenour. I dreaded the fact that I was going to have to go through this same agony every week until the "Pacing Units" deployed.

General Izenour saved the day. He also taught me a lesson. He took one cursory look at what he immediately named "this crap "and told me to scrap it all. He told me to tell it the way it was, to save the creativity, imagination, innovation, etc., for a time when it could accomplish some useful purpose. He said, "If you put all your ideas into this first report, what are you going to do for next week's? And the following week's? Those people are going to want more new ideas every week until all these units get deployed. So, let's start by telling them only what we are actually doing. For units that we haven't activated yet tell them we'll get the people there and handle problems as they occur. We'll be imaginative and creative when we have to be."

My memory has undoubtedly not retained his exact words, but their substance, their lesson, remain. The report I wrote that Sunday was easily and quickly done. General Izenour approved it Monday morning. Wagstaff was not pleased with it. Particularly, since he got essentially the same theme from the equipment people. The unit activation and training people came forth with a tidbit to demonstrate their desire to cooperate with the Secretary. They offered to look into shortening the already accelerated unit training times and into moving up the activation dates. In the face of our collective attitude Wagstaff and his "Indians" could only threaten us with what they predicted would be the unhappy reaction of Mr. Resor.

No thunderbolt struck from on high. I could approach the preparation of the next report in a much more relaxed manner.

Very quickly the Secretary's special "Pacing Unit" report became just another element in our office routine. After the first several I no longer bothered to get either Colonel Mowery's or General Izenour's approval before submitting it to Colonel Wagstaff. Neither asked to see what I was proposing. It was not long before Colonel Wagstaff got the report changed to biweekly. Then, after another four to six weeks, to a monthly. Finally, even before all the units had deployed, he got the report cancelled. And well before that moment Mr. Resor had lost interest in it as well as in the "Pacing Units."

We, on the other hand, had not lost interest in them. We did whatever had to be done to find the people for them. We eventually deployed them on and in some cases, ahead of the originally scheduled dates except for one bitter failure, which I discuss below. They undoubtedly should have been deployed earlier, as the Secretary wanted, but the realities of the situation simply made it impossible. Mr. Resor undoubtedly knew that already when he exhorted us to do better, to overcome those realities. He was very probably receiving the same sort of exhortations from his higher ups, to which he had to respond or, at least, to give the impression that he was responding positively. We in ODCSPER did come up with one innovative approach to expediting the departure of some of the "Pacing Units." It unfortunately proved to be of no avail. The Engineer construction battalions for which we created the approach departed many months after their scheduled dates. Their fate represents the only real failure of Colonel Wagstaff's committee and the Army to meet the deployment requirements requested by General Westmoreland and approved by the Department of Defense.

Chapter 19

The Engineer Construction Battalions

THE Engineer construction battalions were the epitome of a "Pacing Unit." They were the builders of the camps, the roads, the bunkers, etc. There were already a goodly number of them in Vietnam. We activated about a dozen additional ones in 1966 for deployment in early 1967. From the training point of view it could not have been any earlier, regardless of the urgency of the need, because of the length of even their accelerated training program. Regardless of, or maybe because of, their criticality they posed a serious problem for us. We had run out of the right kinds of people to put into them. The most serious lack was Captains. These were the company commanders, the battalion staff officers, on whose experience and knowledge the effective functioning of the units depended. We couldn't throw in miscellaneous captains from other branches. We needed captains who had some idea of what building buildings, constructing roads, laying out airfields, etc., meant. We would have settled for experienced Corps of Engineer first lieutenants, but they were also in short supply. We only needed about 70 of these Captains. Yet in an Army nearing the one million mark we apparently didn't have any. Therefore, we made them.

With the approval of my bosses, I had all the records of all the captains in the Army screened to find those who had civil engineering degrees and were not already Engineer officers. We excluded West Point graduates. We didn't believe the engineering education in their degrees was appropriate for the assignments. We excluded those who were more critically needed where they were, e.g., those already in Vietnam, those already in units going to Vietnam, those who were, or were training, to become, helicopter pilots, those teaching Engineer officers and enlisted men at The Engineer School. We found about 40. We didn't ask for volunteers. We sent each of them a letter stating that he was being detailed to the Corps of Engineers for two years and was being reassigned to the Umpty-umpth Engineer Construction Battalion. The fact that a particular officer had just returned from Vietnam did not affect the assignment, since the battalions would be undergoing a lengthy period of Stateside training before deploying.

As I was reporting our progress in finding and moving the people into these construction battalions my ODCSLOG counterpart on Wagstaff's committee was reporting that the equipment would be in place when the people got there. Engineer construction battalions require a lot of specialized, bulky, heavy, earthmoving, road grading, road surfacing, and material handling equipment. The production lead times on much of this equipment exceeded a year. Consequently, if the units were to deploy on schedule, their equipment would have to be furnished from existing stocks. The ODCSLOG representative assured the committee, and the committee assured the Secretary of the Army in oral and written reports chopped by the DCSLOG, that the equipment would be there.

One day there came into my office a lieutenant colonel from ODCSLOG to get a chop on some document. We had done business together before. We had made a couple of trips together as members of the Department of the Army Readiness Team. We chatted. Why the subject entered the conversation I no longer remember. We talked about the construction battalions. He told me that it was impossible to equip them. He said there wasn't any equipment being manufactured for the Army, there wasn't any equipment in the depots, there wasn't any equipment in the Reserves and National Guard. All of the available equipment had been used to equip the construction battalions already sent to Vietnam. When I asked why the official ODCSLOG representative continued to report that the equipment would be delivered on schedule, he couldn't even surmise a reason. I didn't announce my news at the next meeting of the committee. I did ask, however, whether or not we in ODCSPER could be assured that, if we took exceptional measures to put people into these units, the equipment for them to train on and deploy with would also be there on time. The ODCSLOG representative returned to the next day's meeting to report that the equipment would be there. I couldn't believe it. After the meeting I took him aside and passed to him the information I had without naming my source.

Several meetings later he again reported that the equipment would be delivered. I took my concerns to Lieutenant Colonel "Sam" Houston, Wagstaff's chief "Indian." He queried ODCSLOG through his contacts. The answer was the same: the equipment would be there. The people arrived on time. The equipment did not. When I left the Pentagon in the summer of 1967 the "Pacing" engineer construction battalions were still in the United States. In the spring of 1967 the Department of the Army Readiness Team visited Fort Lewis, Washington, the home of several of these construction battalions. Six or more months after the units had received their personnel they were not able to initiate the requisite training programs because their engineer equipment had not yet arrived. In the units' briefings for the Team the officers expressed their frustrations with poorly concealed undertones of bitterness. They were not a happy group. They had questions to which we could not give truthful answers. We had answers, but since they would have had to reflect stupidity, mendacity, timorousness, and self interest on the part of the Army hierarchy, honesty was not a policy we could adopt. I didn't have to answer their tough, nasty questions about the equipment. It was unpleasant enough trying to justify reassigning people from Europe and elsewhere in the United States on short notice to spend month after month in Fort Lewis twiddling their thumbs.

About nine months after the activation of the units we in ODCSPER decided that we would take out of the battalions those captains we had arbitrarily detailed to the Corps of Engineers and assign them to Vietnam as individual replacements. The Army was still short Engineer Captains. The construction battalions were obviously not going to deploy in the foreseeable future. By this time even the DCSLOG was admitting that the equipment was not available. We felt that we needed to get at least one year's productive service as Engineer officers from those captains we had uprooted to meet what we had been told was an emergency requiring extraordinary measures. We also started taking other people out of these battalions to fill shortages in Vietnam. We even began assigning Vietnam returnees to them since we had become pretty sure that they would not be deploying before these returnees became eligible for reassignment to Vietnam.

By the time the Secretary of the Army's personal interest in the "Pacing Units" had died, the long enduring crises in the preparation of units to deploy to Vietnam had also faded away. During the hectic months of that first year the Department of the Army Committee on Deployments to Vietnam, what I always think of as "Wagstaff's committee," had transformed its reactions to events into a system with rules, norms, and procedures, albeit largely unwritten. The need, almost every day, to improvise, to bend, even break, the old rules no longer existed. Our improvisations had become the rules of a totally revamped system. Difficulties had, of course, not disappeared. The basic problem in supporting the war in Vietnam remained immutable and unmitigated: the Reserves and the National Guard had not been mobilized. I do not wish to imply that had the President mobilized them we would have won the war. I doubt very seriously that their presence on active duty would have altered the outcome in any way, since this resulted primarily from a lack of understanding by our political and military leadership of the true nature of the conflict. They failed to develop and carry out a political and military program that reflected the realities of the conflict. The war disintegrated into a campaign of killing and destruction without strategic purpose. The Reserves and National Guard would not have changed that. Their absence did, however, create difficulties in supporting the war that almost overwhelmed the Army during the initial phases of the buildup. Their absence meant that the war had to be supported by hundreds of thousands of Privates fresh out of basic training and by thousands of Second Lieutenants fresh from Officer Candidate

School. But even these hordes of inexperienced and relatively unskilled soldiers did not become immediately available to meet the immediate soaring demand to put a field army into operation in Vietnam. It took time to open the training centers to receive the draftees. It took time to put the cadres and equipment into these centers. Eventually the numbers caught up with the needs. The quality never did. The problem remained that Privates and Second Lieutenants were required to perform Sergeants' and Captains jobs. Rapidly promoted First Lieutenants were pushed into Majors jobs. There were more than enough Lieutenant Colonels, Colonels, and Generals.

Chapter 20

Postlude

MY reassignment from the Pentagon was as unexpected as my assignment had been. After completing only two years of a normal three year assignment I was shipped off to command a battalion. Someone in the Field Grade Officer Assignment Branch had suddenly discovered that I was about to become eligible for promotion to Colonel, but that I had not yet had a battalion command, the sine qua non for promotion. I left the Pentagon in August 1967, never to return. I was not the only one departing. General Izenour left several months before I did to take over the command of the 2nd Infantry Division in Korea as a newly promoted Major General. Larry Mowery had got himself assigned to the 101st Airborne Division as the Support Command Commander. The 101st had just been alerted for deployment to Vietnam to join its one brigade that had been one of the first combat units there.

Larry thought it would be a fitting tribute to our efforts, or at least, an appropriate going away present, if a grateful Army were to award us the Legion of Merit. A year earlier he had had the same thought with regard to my predecessor, John Kiser. I labored for weeks to prepare the justification for his award. I had seen my first effort bounced back as inadequate to support the award. (Although hundreds of Legions of Merit are awarded every year, most of them are presented to retiring colonels. The award to them is so routine that the decoration is commonly referred to as a Colonel's Good Conduct Medal. When it is awarded under different circumstances, and especially to officers under the rank of Colonel, it retains the significance of its original purpose: to recognize and reward exceptionally meritorious performance of duty.) I rewrote the justification. I even consulted John Kiser himself to obtain information on his accomplishments prior to the time of my arrival. My rewrite did the job. John got his Legion of Merit when he departed.

Mowery felt that he and I and Paul Elliot, the other branch chief, also being reassigned, deserved the Legion of Merit more than John had. So he had Paul write a justification for mine, he had General Izenour's deputy instruct me to write one for him, and he wrote one for Paul. I'm sure he had also greased the skids with General Izenour, whose approval and recommendation were essential. Unfortunately, by the time the justifications were ready to be submitted General Izenour had departed. His replacement, whose name I forget, did not know us. He had no idea of what had been accomplished during the preceding two years. He certainly did not think the accomplishments were of such a magnitude to warrant the award of 3 Legions of Merit at the same time to 3 officers in the same staff division. He, therefore, knocked down the requests to a less meritorious decoration. Larry and Paul, irate, insisted that the requests for them be withdrawn. I did not. I no longer remember why. Perhaps I felt that another decoration, however minor, to add to my meager collection would enhance my chances for promotion. I, therefore, duly received my award.

Six years later, when it came my turn to retire and to receive my Legion of Merit as a retiring Colonel, I asked my boss not to submit the standard request. I told him that I had been refused one the only time in my career when I felt that I had merited it. I didn't want a cheap one. He, nonetheless, had a request prepared and submitted. Approval was automatic. After I had retired, my boss called me at home to request that I come in to the headquarters to receive it. I declined. Several months later I received it by mail.

I do not know what became of my colleagues on the Deployment Committee. I never saw any of them again after I left the Pentagon, except Colonel Wagstaff. Like General Izenour, Colonel Wagstaff left several months before I did. Also like General Izenour he left with a promotion. He finally became the Brigadier General he had worked so diligently to achieve and was assigned to command a unit headquartered in Heidelberg, Germany. I saw him there in the spring of 1967. I was once again with the Department of the Army Unit Readiness Team on its annual visit to USAREUR Headquarters and units in Germany. General Wagstaff's unit was the first one we visited. The visit was to start with a briefing from the general and his staff. The team and the staff gathered after lunch in a conference room to await the general. His aide finally appeared in the doorway to announce, "Gentlemen, the Commanding General." Wagstaff walked into the room. He stopped. His eyes began to search the room. He asked several times, "Where is he?" He finally spotted me in one of the far corners of the room, murmured, "There he is," and began a tour of the room to greet each of the team members. His greeting to me was not out of the ordinary. When we were all at last seated around the conference table he began the meeting with an announcement. I no longer remember his exact words, but their substance remains embedded in my memory. He launched into a concise description of what the Army's Committee for Unit Deployments to Vietnam was and what it had accomplished. "Lieutenant Colonel Landis and three or four others were the life blood of that committee during its most critical moments. Without their efforts the Committee would not have succeeded, nor the Army met its requirements to support the war in Vietnam. The fact that I am a general officer is solely a result of the accomplishments of that committee. Colonel Landis was not able to attend my farewell party in the Pentagon where I expressed my indebtedness to his colleagues and to him. I wish to take this opportunity to acknowledge publicly and in his presence that I owe my stars to Colonel Landis. Ben, I thank you."

I was dumfounded. I could think of nothing to say. The meeting proceeded without further ado. In all of my service, previous and subsequent, at the many promotion parties I attended did I ever hear another officer, general or other, give credit for his promotion to any person by name other than his wife and children. Whenever I think of Wagstaff's little speech, as I occasionally do, the memory kindles a feeling of pride that no Legion of Merit could. Brigadier General Wagstaff moved up to the rank of Major General before retiring. Whether any of his assignments as a general had the same importance as his last assignment as a colonel, I do not know.

I saw General Wagstaff once more many years later after we had both retired. It was at a large cocktail party. I happened to see him just as his wife and he were leaving. I went over to say hello. I introduced myself. He didn't seem to have the slightest idea who I was.

Colonel Mowery commanded a brigade in the 101st Airborne Division in Vietnam, as well as the Division Support Command. Upon his return from Vietnam he was assigned to the faculty at The Infantry School at Fort Benning, Georgia. He retired as a Colonel. Of all the officers I knew in my career, Colonel Larry Mowery was among the most qualified to be a general officer. Among all the Colonels I knew, he was undoubtedly the best qualified to be a general officer. That the Army's politics prevented his designation was a real loss to the United States Army.

John Kiser retired as a Colonel and moved into the Virginia hinterlands. Until his much-too-early death, we exchanged Christmas cards and saw each other every couple of years in his Virginia hideaway. In his home he still had the statuette of that red cat that I first saw in his office. Then it was the sole decoration in a drab environment; in his home it clashed with its tasteful surroundings. Only a few of his visitors probably knew that it was not just an ugly artifact but a symbol of the United States Army's Unit Readiness System, which John and I helped to direct in its infancy.

Colonel Lawrence L. Mowery, Chief, Distribution and Readiness Division, Directorate for Procurement and Distribution, Office of the Deputy Chief of Staff, Personnel, Headquarters, U.S. Army.

Lieutenant General James K. Woolnough, USA, Deputy Chief of Staff, Personnel.

General Creighton W. Abrams, USA, Vice Chief of Staff, U.S. Army.

General Harold K. Johnson, USA, Chief of Staff, U.S. Army.

Colonel Jack J. Wagstaff, USA, Division Chief, Office of the Deputy Chief of Staff, Operations, Headquarters, U.S. Army.

Brigadier General Frank M. Izenour, Director, Directorate for Procurement and Distribution, Office of the Deputy Chief of Staff, Personnel, Headquarters, U.S. Army.

Hon. Stanley R. Resor, Secretary of the Army.

Lieutenant Colonel John B. Kiser, Chief, Readiness Branch, Distribution and Readiness Division, Directorate for Procurement and Distribution, Office of the Deputy Chief of Staff, Personnel, Headuqarters, U.S. Army.

The author, 1951.

The author receiving the Soldier's Medal for heroism froim the Deputy Chief of Staff, Operations, Headquarters, U.S. Army Europe, 1963.

*AR 220-1

ARMY REGULATION } HEADQUARTERS
No. 220-1 DEPARTMENT OF THE ARMY
WASHINGTON, D.C., *20 February 1967*

FIELD ORGANIZATIONS

UNIT READINESS

Effective with the 20 June 1967 Report

		Paragraph	Page
SECTION I.	GENERAL PROVISIONS		
	Purpose	1	2
	Scope	2	2
	Headquarters reporting to Headquarters, Department of the Army	3	2
	Definitions	4	2
	Objectives of the readiness system	5	3
	Readiness requirement (REDCAT)	6	3
	Readiness capability (REDCAPE)	7	4
	Exception units	8	5
	Unit Readiness Report	9	5
	Readiness levels	10	6
II.	PREPARATION OF DA FORM 2715		
	Unit Readiness Report (Reports Control Symbol CSGPO-266(R2))	11	7
	DA Form 2715 (Unit Readiness Report)	12	7
III.	PUNCHED CARDS		
	Preparation	13	10
IV.	PREPARATION OF MAJOR COMMAND SUMMARY EVALUATION		
	Major Command Summary Evaluation of Unit Readiness (Reports Control Symbol CSGPO-265(R2))	14	14
V.	LOGISTICS ANALYSIS OF MAJOR ARMY COMMAND SUMMARY EVALUATION		
	Instructions	15	17
APPENDIX A.	REDCAT/REDCAPE LEVELS	--	19
B.	REDCON CRITERIA	--	20
C.	PERSONNEL	--	23
D.	TRAINING	--	25
E.	LOGISTICS	--	31
F.	ADDRESSEES FOR COMMANDERS SUMMARY EVALUATIONS	--	41
G.	REFERENCES	--	43

---

*After 1 April 1967 this regulation supersedes AR 220-1, 28 July 1965, including C 3, 5 January 1966, and AR 750-10, 28 July 1965 except as AR 750-10 applies to Reserve and National Guard units reporting under AR 135-8.

TAGO 6875A

IMPROVISING A WAR 143

AR 220-1

Section I. GENERAL PROVISIONS

1. **Purpose.** This regulation establishes uniform readiness standards and reporting procedures which are designed to assist Headquarters, Department of the Army (DA) and commanders at all levels in making the most effective use of available resources and in determining requirements for additional resources.

2. **Scope.** The provisions of this regulation are applicable to all major Army commands, to all Table of Organization and Equipment (TOE) units of the Active Army except those specifically exempted, to certain Table of Distribution and Allowance (TDA) units designated by major Army commanders as reporting units, and to National Guard Air Defense Artillery Missile units which are "on-site" within the United States. Units preparing for deployment to an active combat theater will discontinue reporting under this regulation upon reaching their Personnel on Station Date (POSD) unless otherwise directed by Department of the Army. Units will then commence reporting under AR 220-10. Units engaged in combat operations in South Vietnam are excused from the reporting requirements contained herein unless otherwise directed by Department of the Army.

3. **Headquarters reporting to Headquarters, Department of the Army.** For purposes of this regulation, the following major Army commands are designated reporting commands to Headquarters, Department of the Army: The U.S. Continental Army Command (USCONARC); U.S. Army Combat Developments Command (USACDC); U.S. Army Air Defense Command (ARADCOM); U.S. Army, Alaska (USARAL); U.S. Army, Europe (USAREUR); U.S. Army, Pacific (USARPAC); U.S. Army Forces Southern Command (USARSO); U.S. Army Security Agency (USASA); and the U.S. Army Strategic Communications Command (USASTRATCOM). In addition, the Army Map Service is designated a reporting command. Other major Army commands, although not reporting, will establish authorization levels under procedures set forth in AR 310-44. In order to understand fully the requirements of this regulation, it is essential that commanders and staff become familiar with applicable references which are listed in appendix G.

4. **Definitions.** *a. Readiness requirement (REDCAT).* The level of required readiness assigned to each unit of a command for the accomplishment of assigned missions.

b. Readiness capability (REDCAPE). The level of readiness assigned to each unit of a command which is within the capability of the major Army command to support with personnel spaces and equipment items on hand and programed for the command.

c. Readiness condition (REDCON). The actual level of readiness of a unit at a particular time.

d. Full TOE. The personnel and equipment shown in the full strength columns of DA published TOE, including DA numbered changes, plus or minus DA directed or approved additions or deletions for operational purposes. Additions or deletions required for non-TOE missions in support of local garrison or other peacetime missions are excluded from the computation of "full TOE." These requirements, if authorized, will be authorized by TDA. Full TOE for a unit is the 100 percent requirement of personnel and equipment for sustained operations under its stated TOE mission, and as such would accompany the unit when deployed or committed. Specifically full TOE is based on—

(1) The full column of Sections II and III of TOE with suffix "F" or earlier and "T" tables in the same format; level 1 column of modified TOE (MTOE); or level 1 columns of Sections II and III of TOE with suffix "G" or later and "T" tables in the same format (see AR 310-31). For units composed of two or more cells from cellular TOE, full TOE require-

AR 220-1

ments are determined from the summation of the personnel and equipment paragraphs for the teams and/or individual spaces included in the cellular organization. By MTOE action, delete unnecessary personnel spaces from TOE teams when sufficient personnel for the unit's mission are present in other cells of the unit. When spaces are deleted, the corresponding items of equipment will also be deleted from full TOE computations for composite cellular units. Normally, the total of the combined cells in a cellular unit will be something less than the full total of all of the cells involved.

(2) Department of the Army directed or approved modifications for operational purposes.

(3) Department of the Army approved use of augmentation paragraphs.

e. Authorized strength. The total military personnel spaces authorized in manpower documents. It is that strength in terms of military personnel spaces provided to man the Army, command, or agency at a given structure based on TOE/MTOE and TDA/MTDA as approved by Headquarters, Department of the Army.

f. Accountable strength. All military personnel assigned by competent orders to the reporting unit regardless of duty station. Includes personnel who are present for duty, absent from duty, intransit-incoming, and intransit-outgoing.

g. Operating strength. Present and absent military strength of an organization classified under the item "personnel status" of the morning report heading as "permanent party." Does not include intransit or attached strength.

h. Deployable strength. Military personnel included in the operating strength and deployable under current criteria.

i. Gains and losses. Military personnel added to or lost from the operating strength during the reporting quarter.

j. Resources.

(1) *Actual.* For purposes of readiness reporting, actual resources are military personnel (operating strength) and equipment on hand.

(2) *Programed.* For purposes of recommending and approving REDCAPE, programed resources are Program and Budget Guidance military space authorizations and forecast equipment for which MILSTRIP information or delivery advice has been received.

5. Objectives of the readiness system. The primary objectives of the Army readiness system are to insure that each unit has its authorized personnel with the required skills available for duty; that its authorized equipment is on hand and maintained in an operational condition; that its needed supplies are on hand; and that each unit is maintaining a state of training which will permit accomplishment of the mission reflected in the authorization document under which it is organized. Effectively utilized and supervised, the system will permit Department of the Army to accomplish the following:

a. Provide a basis for orderly distribution of actual and programed resources.

b. Provide justification for requesting additional programed resources from the Department of Defense.

c. Determine Army-wide and command-wide readiness trends.

d. Identify readiness problems which require resolution.

6. Readiness requirement (REDCAT). *a.* REDCAT for individual units represent the total requirements for personnel and equipment for best accomplishment of assigned missions. REDCAT are derived from general war and contingency plans, including the deployment schedules associated with those plans; from the vulnerability of units to attack by potential enemies; and from other operational tasks assigned major Army commanders by higher authority (app A). All TOE and TDA units are assigned an individual REDCAT (except organic elements of divisions, armored cavalry regiments, DA-designated separate brigades, and separate nondivisional battalions). On-site air defense units will be assigned REDCAT by individual battery and Special Forces units by individual company. REDCAT assignment for TDA units will be C1 and will be based on requirements columns of authorization documents.

b. The actual resource requirements (military personnel and equipment) necessary to match REDCON with REDCAT for all Army TOE/MTOE units plus the requirements for TDA/MTDA units approximates the total current Army unit requirements for military personnel and equipment, exclusive of modernization items. These data assist Department of the Army in preparation of the Army budget and justification for military space authorization to the Department of Defense. Attainment of approved REDCAT for every unit in the Army is the overall readiness objective. Normally, this REDCAT is full TOE (level 1) at time of deployment or employment. Major Army commanders forward recommended REDCAT for assigned units to Department of the Army for approval. The approved REDCAT are then used by Department of the Army and major Army commanders to determine resource requirements and express shortfalls. REDCAT for individual units are unclassified, but a list of command-wide REDCAT will be classified CONFIDENTIAL.

7. Readiness capability (REDCAPE). a. In order to retain the true requirements (REDCAT) as an objective, while at the same time conducting the day-to-day business with the resources made available to the Army by higher authority, a level of readiness for each unit is established which is within the capability of the Army to support with programed personnel spaces (by identity) and equipment—this is the unit REDCAPE.

b. Major Army commanders recommend REDCAPE for all TOE and TDA units of their command, insuring that the total of military personnel spaces (by identity) and equipment necessary to support REDCAPE equals the total of such resources programed for the command. This is the means by which personnel spaces and equipment programed for the command are identified and distributed. REDCAPE is the highest level of readiness for individual units within the programed capability of the major Army commander to support. REDCAPE are recommended and approved for all TOE and TDA units (less organic elements of divisions, armored cavalry regiments, DA-designated separate brigades and separate nondivisional battalions). TDA units approved to report under this regulation by Headquarters, Department of the Army will be assigned REDCAPE based on authorized military strength. TDA units will report using authorized strengths as full TOE. On-site air defense units will be recommended by battery for REDCAPE assignment and Special Forces units by company.

c. Major Army commanders will forward unit REDCAPE recommendations to Headquarters, Department of the Army for approval. It is Department of the Army intent that TOE units be organized so far as possible, at levels 1 (REDCAPE C1), 2 (REDCAPE C2), or 3 (REDCAPE C3). Exceptions to this policy are contained in paragraph 8. Review and approval of a unit REDCAPE for a specified level of authorization by Department of the Army signifies that personnel and equipment are authorized and are programed as of a given date. Department of the Army approval of recommended REDCAPE signifies an intention to support the unit concerned with actual resources adequate to permit attainment of a comparable REDCON. REDCAPE approval establishes the level of authorization for the unit and the requirements for the personnel and equipment distribution of actual assets to meet the authorized level. Approved REDCAPE also establishes the immediate readiness objective for the unit commander.

d. Major Army commanders update REDCAPE recommendations by submission of authorization documents (AR 310–31 and AR

AR 220-1

310-49) in accordance with AR 11-15. This action is accomplished on a continuing basis in order to insure that troop bases are in agreement with the latest Department of the Army published Program and Budget Guidance as supplemented or amended by subsequent Department of the Army directives. A basic requirement for the Army's readiness system is that the authorized level of organization of all TOE units in the Army plus TDA/MTDA authorizations be balanced with Department of Defense allocated manpower spaces (by identity) and with logistics resources. REDCAPE adjustments are required when the major commander can predict programed changes in authorizations or when program and budget guidance is changed.

e. REDCAPE for individual units are UNCLASSIFIED, but a list of command-wide REDCAPE will be classified CONFIDENTIAL.

f. REDCAPE for units in Korea will be established based on the authorization of U.S. personnel without consideration of KATUSA augmentations. Although not considered when assigning unit REDCAPE, MTOE for such units will authorize additional individual and unit equipment to equip assigned KATUSA personnel.

g. REDCAPE cannot be used for expressing desired requirements, but must express what can be supported. Since REDCAPE are contingent upon the personnel spaces and equipment resources programed for a command, a shortage in either area can cause a reduction in the REDCAPE recommended for a specific unit with the lower capability determining the overall REDCAPE. So far as equipment is concerned, REDCAPE must be predicated upon a major Army commander's reportable equipment to include that programed. The objective is to achieve a balanced organization at each level. This is the structure that provides the personnel, in the proper numbers and skills, required to utilize effectively the equipment authorized. Temporary deferment in modernization of equipment should not be considered in recommending REDCAPE. The latest available program documents should be used and equipment availability programs should be extended so far as possible, along with personnel programs, in order to achieve the optimum prediction of resource availability.

8. Exception units. Major Army commanders may request exception to Department of the Army organizational policy at levels 1, 2, or 3 for organization of units when required because of current peacetime missions. Exceptions will be confined to units whose peacetime mission permits an organization at less than level 3 of the published TOE, but whose wartime requirements necessitate an increase in personnel and equipment. An example of this type of unit is a replacement battalion stationed in an inactive oversea theater. Requests for exception units, with justification on an individual unit basis, will be forwarded to Department of the Army. When reporting REDCON for exception units, Department of the Army approved authorizations (peacetime level at which organized) will be substituted as full TOE (level 1) strength/equipment. Exception units will be assigned REDCAT C1, based on combat operational requirements and REDCAPE "E" at the level of authorization.

9. Unit Readiness Report. *a.* The Unit Readiness Report (DA Form 2715) (RCS CSGPO-266 (R2)) required by this regulation provides a means for commanders to identify problem areas in personnel, training, and logistics where command emphasis and/or corrective action may be required. To insure a uniform report, full TOE (strength and equipment) discussed in paragraph 4*d* is used as the basic standard of measurement for all TOE units other than *exception* units. Authorized levels are used for reporting TDA units and *exception* units:

b. When computing the readiness of medical units, the following will apply:

(1) *For STRAF medical units.* The Surgeon General (TSG) will maintain a listing of AMEDS officers (OTSG fillers) eligible for assignment to STRAF units. Filler personnel will be provided by TSG when a STRAF unit

AR 220-1

is selected for a mission requiring full TOE staffing. When determining the REDCON of a STRAF medical unit, all AMEDS officers requirements and assets will be considered as available. Commanders responsible for reporting the readiness of zero strength STRAF medical units will also consider earmarked enlisted personnel as available assets for reporting purposes. The status and serviceability of equipment on hand or earmarked for zero strength STRAF medical units will be included in the readiness report.

(2) *For all other medical units.* Operating personnel plus those AMEDS officers and enlisted personnel who are earmarked for assignment to the reporting unit upon alert, deployment or initiation of a combat mission will be considered as available when determining the personnel REDCON. Critical medical personnel on the Post M-Day Deployment List (PMDL) will not be considered as available for reporting UAREUR medical units. Oversea commanders responsible for providing earmarked AMEDS personnel will provide feeder information, to include POR and MOS qualification of designees, to the reporting commanders no later than 15 days prior to the end of the reporting period, to permit reporting unit commanders to include the information in quarterly readiness reports. The earmarking of resources will not be duplicated by the allocation of personnel or equipment to more than one reporting unit. Personnel assigned to a reporting medical unit who, under alert, deployment, or combat conditions, are designated for reassignment to another unit, will be reported by the unit for which earmarked.

c. When the measured REDCON balances the assigned REDCAPE, the unit is considered to be in a readiness condition which is commensurate with current allocated resources. Since REDCON deficiencies pinpoint problem areas, discrepancies between REDCAPE and the reported REDCON will initially call for examination of the procedures being used by the unit to manage actual resources or for reexamination of the allocation of these resources to the unit by the major Army commander. Consistent discrepancies call for reexamination of resource allocation and reporting procedures by Headquarters, Department of the Army.

d. It is important that unit readiness reports reflect the true condition of a unit. Corrective action should be directed if a unit commander has not complied with applicable regulations and has not made full use of resources available to him. However, if the unit commander has complied with regulations and has exhausted the resources at his disposal and the objective factors on which the readiness report is based indicate that his unit readiness condition (REDCON) is below its assigned readiness capability (REDCAPE), no higher commander in the chain of command will consider this fact as reflecting unfavorably upon the unit commander.

10. **Readiness levels.** The unit commander determines the REDCON based on his knowledge of conditions within the unit. In order that REDCON be measured objectively and uniformly, common factors in the areas of personnel, training, and logistics have been selected as readiness indicators. The criteria for determining the unit REDCON levels described below are contained in appendix B.

a. *REDCON C1.* Unit is fully capable of performing the full TOE mission for which organized or designed.

b. *REDCON C2.* Unit is capable of performing the full TOE mission for which organized or designed, but has minor deficiencies which reduce its ability to conduct sustained operations.

c. *REDCON C3.* Unit has deficiencies of such magnitude as to limit its capability to perform the full TOE mission for which organized or designed, but is capable nonetheless of conducting operations for a limited period.

6

AGO 6875A

AR 220-1

d. REDCON C4. Unit has deficiencies of such magnitude as to limit severely its capability to perform the full TOE mission for which it is organized or designed.

Section II. PREPARATION OF DA FORM 2715

11. **Unit Readiness Report (Reports Control Symbol CSGPO-266 (R2)).** This report consists of two parts: DA Form 2715 (Unit Readiness Report) and 80-column, general purpose, punched cards (para 13).

a. Preparing DA Form 2715. This form will be prepared, as prescribed below, by unit commanders "as of" 21 March, 20 June, 20 September, and 21 December or 10 days prior to the end of each FY quarter. Reports will be classified CONFIDENTIAL as a minimum. Headquarters, Department of the Army requirements for submitting reports include all numbered TOE units, company-size or larger; all TOE Military Intelligence units, detachments and larger, except CONUS based Military Intelligence groups; and designated TDA units. TDA units reporting under this regulation will be as recommended by designated commanders (para 3) reporting to the Department of the Army and as approved by Headquarters, Department of the Army. Organic subordinate units of divisions, armored cavalry regiments, and DA-designated separate brigades and battalions are not required to report to Headquarters, Department of the Army individually since consolidated division/regiment/brigade/separate battalion reports only are required. However, DA Form 2715 may be used as a feeder report to support consolidated reports.

b. Special instructions.

(1) *On-site missile units (Active Army and National Guard).*
   (a) Report by headquarters battery and individual fire units.
   (b) NIKE HERC double batteries will report as a single unit.

(2) *Special Forces units.* Report by company.

(3) *Units organized without a parent battalion (Example: A Co, 40th Armor).* Report by company.

(4) *All other letter designated units.* Do not report individually.

(5) *Headquarters units whose subordinate units report individually.* Do not submit a consolidated report but only unit report.

(6) *Intermediate commands.* Subject to requirements of the command reports control system, intermediate commands may add summaries, consolidate reports, or require reports from units other than those prescribed above. Increased reporting frequency or additional data may be prescribed as required to meet the needs of commands.

12. **DA Form 2715 (Unit Readiness Report).**
a. Format.

(1) *Heading.*
   (a) *As of.* "As of" date.
   (b) *To.* As prescribed by major command.
   (c) *Thru.* As prescribed by using Army commands. Reports may be forwarded through channels and consolidated at echelons required by major commands.
   (d) *From.* Unit number, designation, and station of the unit for which prepared.
   (e) *Major command code.* See paragraph 13.
   (f) *Unit Identification Code.* See paragraph 13.
   (g) *Aggregate full TOE strength.* See paragraphs 4d and 13.
   (h) *REDCAT.* Readiness requirement assigned to the reporting unit.
   (i) *REDCAPE.* Readiness capability assigned to the reporting unit.
   (j) *Unit structure indicator and exception unit percentage.* See paragraph 13.

AGO 6975A

7

AR 220-1

(2) *Sections A, B, and C.* For each item, enter a single digit in the blocks provided to indicate the correct readiness condition code as determined from the criteria in appendix B. Enter the letter N in blocks not applicable to the reporting unit. In the area headed by block 23 (Strength), the full TOE, authorized, accountable, deployable (CONUS units and oversea long tour areas) and operating strengths of the unit by officers, warrant officers, and enlisted men will be entered. In the area headed by block 35 (MOS), the percent of full TOE strength who are qualified to perform the duties to which assigned will be entered. In the additional space in block 35 gains/losses will be shown in two columns: A—Department of the Army gains/losses (replacements, levy, rotation, ETS, deaths and desertions) and, B—Command gains/losses (e.g., reassignments). Commanders may make additional entries in the areas headed by the other REDCON blocks such as—

(a) Inspections—date and rating of last inspection.

(b) Explanation when, because of the categorical nature of the system, the REDCON rating does not fully reflect all of the significant factors affecting the true readiness condition.

(c) Explanation of any other factor not covered in the report form which has an effect on the readiness condition of the unit.

(3) *Section D (overall REDCON).*

(a) In order to determine a meaningful overall unit REDCON and to permit the unit to be credited with its balance of unit loads on hand, compute the single unit load REDCON (app E). Then, considering the REDCON ratings in blocks 23, 35, 50–56, 63, and 71 along with the computed single unit load REDCON (block 70), enter the lowest rating in block 72. This becomes the overall unit REDCON.

(b) Space is provided for a unit commander to specify needs in personnel, skills, equipment, training, funds (if applicable), relief from obstacles to training, and training facilities to raise his unit to its assigned REDCAPE. Any unusual problems indicated in Sections A, B, or C will be explained. Comments will be continued on additional pages if necessary and will include the following, as appropriate:

1. MOS shortages which jeopardize units' capability to perform its TOE/TDA mission.
2. Number of assigned personnel undergoing BCT/AIT with the unit.
3. Number of KATUSA personnel authorized and assigned (Eighth U.S. Army units only).
4. List of repair parts shortages (with requisitioning data) which jeopardize the unit's capability to perform its TOE/TDA mission.
5. Units that send information copies of the report to Department of the Army under the provisions of *c* below will provide, as a part of the first fiscal year quarter report each year, a listing in TOE line item detail showing the authorized and on-hand quantities of each reportable line item (RICC-1). Change information to update these listings will be provided with the three subsequent reports during the fiscal year. Other units will list those TOE reportable line items (RICC-1) which cause an entry in block 55 (Equipment on Hand) to be less than the REDCAPE assigned to the unit (e.g., a unit assigned REDCAPE C2 would list in TOE line item detail the authorized and on-hand quantities of those RICC-1 items at less than 90 percent of "full TOE" at 80 percent fill).

AR 220-1

6. Maintenance problems attributed to funds; technical assistance; facilities; tools; overage equipment; contingency and training type or obsolete types of equipment.
7. Explanation of any other equipment factor not covered in the report which has a significant effect on the readiness condition of a unit, e.g., major equipment reportable (RICC-1) under AR 711-140 and not designated for profiling. In accordance with AR 310-31, TOE documents will identify items to be reported. For TDA units directed to report under this regulation, the TDA proponent will identify items which are essential.
8. The extent to which subordinate units have been "zeroed out" or placed in caretaker status due to personnel shortages. Include recovery dates if projectable.

(4) *Section E.* Entries will be made by the next higher commander who can influence the readiness condition of the unit. He will consider assets within his control available for distribution to the unit in an emergency and within the criteria outlined in appendix B. When the assets available to higher commanders can be used to correct reported deficiencies in the unit, an entry will be made in Section E raising the REDCON so affected. When REDCON are raised, other than as the result of correction of minor errors in the report, explanations to support the changes will be included. The planned use of resources by higher commanders will be controlled to insure the same assets are not applied to more than one unit. If REDCON must be lowered by higher commander, an explanation is required in Section E and/or F. When a subordinate unit does not attain the assigned REDCAPE due to a shortage of funds, such information will be included in this section. Comments regarding actions taken or planned to correct reported deficiencies and/or specific assistance required from the next higher commander should also be included in this section of the report.

(5) *Section F.* Entries will be made by major Army commanders unless authority is delegated to numbered Army commanders under their command. Provisions outlined in the previous paragraph for raising and/or lowering unit REDCON are also applicable.

(6) *Sections E and F.* Because of the organizational structure of ARADCOM, the "next higher commander" and the "Army commander" for readiness reporting purposes will be designated by CGARADCOM.

b. *Forwarding DA Form 2715.* Reports will be forwarded through channels as directed by major Army commanders. National Guard on-site missile units will submit reports through ARADCOM or USARPAC as appropriate. Copies will be furnished State Adjutants General. Special Warfare augmentation units of the Special Action Force will report individually through the unit, command, or agency to which attached at the time of the report. Major Army commanders will establish procedures for forwarding reports to servicing data processing units for preparation of required punched cards.

c. *Direct submission information copies.* As an additional requirement, information copies of DA Form 2715 for the following TOE combat, combat support, and combat service support units (exceptions noted below) will be forwarded by the commander completing Section E direct to Deputy Chief of Staff for Military Operations, ATTN: OPS-OD RE, Department of the Army, Washington, D.C., 20310, so as to arrive not later than the 10th day of the month following the reporting quarter:

(1) Divisions (consolidated division report and a copy of the report from the attached intelligence detachment).
(2) Armored cavalry regiments.
(3) DA-designated separate brigades. (Brigades organized with all subordi-

AR 220-1

nate elements listed in the separate brigade TOE/MTOE.)
(4) Separate nondivisional battalions to include organic elements of non-DA-designated separate brigades, less CDC.
   (a) Infantry (all types; includes Berlin battalions).
   (b) Artillery (less air defense).
   (c) Engineer (construction battalions in CONUS only, combat battalions worldwide).
   (d) Armor.
(5) Aviation companies (including transportation corps and medical helicopter companies) not organic to divisions.

Section III. PUNCHED CARDS

13. **Preparation.** Data recorded on DA Form 2715 and required organizational data will be punched on general purpose cards. Card columns apply, where applicable, to corresponding column numbers preprinted on DA Form 2715. The letter "N" will be punched in columns 18 through 78 when not applicable to a reporting unit.

a. *Format.*

Data	Columns punched	Remarks
(1) Card number	1–3	Sequence number of each detail card within a given report beginning with ∅∅2.
(2) Security classification	4	Enter "C"
(3) Card type	5	Enter "D"
(4) Major command code	6	See note 1.
(5) Unit Identification code	7–12	See note 2.
(6) Aggregate full TOE/TDA strength	13–17	Full TOE/TDA as verified by major Army commander. See note 3.
(7) REDCAT	18	All units.
(8) REDCAPE	19	Do.
(9) Unit Structure Indicator	20	See note 4.
(10) Exception unit percentage	21–22	See note 5.
(11) Strength	23	REDCON Code.
Aggregate operating strength	24–28	CONUS and long tour oversea theaters.
Aggregate deployment strength	30–34	
(12) Military Occupational Specialty	35	REDCON Code.
Department of the Army Gains	36–39	
Losses	40–43	
Command Gains	44–46	
Losses	47–49	
(13) Refresher training	50	REDCON Code.
(14) Squad/Crew proficiency	51	Do.
(Quarterly Operational Readiness Evaluation—Air Defense Missile Units)		
(15) Unit proficiency	52	Do.
(Air Defense Combat Readiness Training Exercise—Air Defense Missile Units)		
(16) Field exercises (TPI—Air Defense Missile Units)	53	Do.

AR 220-1

Data	Columns punched	Remarks
(17) Mission training (Annual Service Practice—Air Defense Missile Units)	54	Do.
(18) Equipment on hand	55	Do.
(19) Unit equipment serviceability	56	Do.
(20) Computed 6-digital profile	57-62	See appendix E.
(21) Unit equipment deployability	63	
(22) Computed 6-digit profile	64-69	See appendix E.
(23) Single unit load REDCON	70	See appendix E.
(24) Command maintenance management inspection	71	REDCON Code.
(25) Unit commander objective evaluation	72	Do.
(26) Higher command evaluation:		
Personnel	73	Do.
Training	74	Do.
Logistics	75	Do.
(27) Army commander evaluation:		
Personnel	76	Do.
Training	77	Do.
(28) Blank	79-80	

Note 1. The following major command codes will apply:

Major command	Code
CONARC/ARSTRIKE	V
USAREUR	E
USARPAC	P
USACDC	D
ARADCOM	R
USARAL	A
USARSO	S
Army Map Service	H
USASA	N
USASTRATCOM	C

Note 2. The unit identification code as specified by AR 18-50 and as listed in AR 18-50-10 will be utilized. When submitting a consolidated report, the UIC of headquarters and headquarters company of the consolidating headquarters will be punched in columns 7 through 10 and "AA" in columns 11 through 12.

Note 3. When the number of columns provided are more than required by the reporting units, "zeros" will be inserted in the unused columns. *Example.* A unit whose aggregate full TOE strength is 91 would be coded 00091 in columns 13 through 17.

Note 4. The unit structure indicator will utilize one of the following codes: (Use also for exception units.)

1—A unit that has been approved by Department of the Army for organization at less than level 3 of published TOE.
2—A unit that is organized less a complete subordinate element.
3—A split unit. A parent unit with organic elements reporting through command channels other than the parent unit.
N—A unit that does not fall into any one or falls into two or more of the above categories.

Note 5. The exception unit percentage will apply to all exception units. The data field will contain the approved percentage for under 80 percent full TOE. *Example.* A unit approved for 73 percent full TOE would be coded 73. The letters "NN" will be used when these columns are not applicable.

AR 220-1

b. *Forwarding punched cards.*

(1) *Card transmission.* Punched cards for reporting units outside the Washington, D.C. area will be transmitted to Commanding Officer, U.S. Army Information and Data Systems Command, CSAIDS-CS, Department of the Army, Washington, D.C. 20310, utilizing the Autodin Network. When Autodin is not available, the cards will be sent direct to USAIDSCOM by registered air mail. Cards will arrive not later than the 30th day of the month following the reporting quarter. (See (5) below for units located in the Washington, D.C. area.) Reports submitted via AUTODIN will consist of the following types of cards:

(a) Communications Header Card.
(b) Security Classification Card.
(c) Report Header Card.
(d) Report Detail Card(s).
(e) Report End Card.
(f) Communications End of Transmission Card.

Reports submitted via registered Air Mail will consist of the Report Header Card, Report Detail Card(s) and the Report End Card only. Card formats are shown in figure 1.

(2) *Card numbering.* Except for the Communications Header and End of Transmission Cards, all cards are numbered in card columns 1–3 as follows:

(a) The Security Classification Card is always numbered 000.
(b) The Report Header Card is always numbered 001.
(c) Report Detail Cards are numbered sequentially within each report beginning with the number 002.
(d) The Report End Card receives the next summer in sequence after the card number of the last Report Detail Card.

(3) *Card type coding.* The Report Header Card, Report Detail Cards, and the Report End Card are all coded in column 5 to indicate the type of cards as follows:

(a) The Report Header Card is always coded "H".
(b) The Report End Card is always coded "E".
(c) Report Detail Cards are always coded "D".

(4) *Card formats.* The format for each type of header and trailer card is as follows:

(a) *Communications Header Card (see JANAP 128A).*

Data	Card Columns	Remarks
Precedence	1	Z = Flash
		O = Immediate
		P = Priority
		R = Routine
Mode of transmission	2–3	CC = Card to card
Security classification	4	E = EFTO
		U = Unclassified
		C = Confidential
		S = Secret
		T = Top Secret
Blank	5	
Content indicator	6–8	Enter "GGA"
Blank	9	

12

AGO 6875A

AR 220-1

Data	Card Columns	Remarks
Submitting agency	10–16	Originators routing indicator as shown in current edition of ACP 117 US SUPP-2.
Message serial number	17–20	Assigned by communications personnel.
Blank	21	
Julian date	22–24	The numbered day of the year (leading zeros will be used).
Time of filing	25–28	Time of filing with communications center expressed as hours and minutes ZULU.
Blank	29	
Total card count	30–33	Total of all cards transmitted including Communications Header and End of Transmission Cards.
12 Punch	34	
Security classification	35–38	Repeat same code used in column 4, four times, i.e., CCCC = Confidential.
12 Punch	39–40	
Addressee routing indicator	41–47	Enter "RUEOEDE"
12-3-8 Punch	48	
Blank	49–80	

(b) *Security Classification Card.*

Data	Card Columns	Remarks
Card number	1–3	Enter ∅∅∅
Blank	4–5	
Security classification	6–28	The security classification of the report (spelled out—not abbreviated).
Blank	29–80	

(c) *Report Header Card.*

Data	Card Columns	Remarks
Card number	1–3	Enter ∅∅∅
Security classification	4	E = EFTO U = Unclassified C = Confidential S = Secret T = Top Secret
Card type	5	Enter "H"
AS-of-time	6–17	Enter appropriate date-time-group of report AS-of-time (e.g., 202400Z Sep 67).
Blank	18	
Format indicator	19	Enter 11-3-8 Punch.
Report type	20–42	Enter "UNIT READINESS AR 220-1".
Originators UIC	70–75	UIC of headquarters originating the report.

AR 220-1

Data	Card Columns	Remarks
Report type	76-77	Enter "RE"
Batch number	78-80	For use with multi-section reports. (*Note.* The maximum number of cards in any one report is 500.) Each batch will carry a separate number beginning with ∅∅1.

(d) *Report End Card.*

Data	Card Columns	Remarks
Cards number	1-3	This will be the next number in sequence following the card number of the last detail card.
Security classification	4	Same as CC4 of the Report Header Card.
Card type	5	Enter "E"
Blank	6-19	
	20-80	Same as CC 20-80 of Report Header Card.

(e) *End of Transmission Card.*

Data	Card Columns	Remarks
	1-38	Same as CC 1-38 of Communications Header Card.
Blank	39-76	
End indicator	77-80	Enter "NNNN"

(5) *Direct submission.* Punched card reports of the following agencies and commands in the Washington, D.C. area will be accompanied by DA Form 200 (Transmittal Record) and will consist of Report Header, Report Detail, and Report End cards only:

USACDC USASA
USASTRATCOM Army Map Service

These reports will be delivered to Commanding Officer, U.S. Army Information and Data Systems Command, Washington, D.C., 20310, so as to arrive not later than the 30th day of the month following the report quarter.

(6) *Multiple Layout Card Form.* See figure 1.

Section IV. PREPARATION OF MAJOR COMMAND SUMMARY EVALUATION

14. **Major Command Summary Evaluation of Unit Readiness (Reports Control Symbol CSGPO-265 (R2)).** *a. General.* Major Army commanders will dispatch a narrative summary evaluation to Deputy Chief of Staff for Military Operations, ATTN: OPS-OD RE, Department of the Army, Washington, D.C., 20310, to arrive by the 15th day of the second month following the end of the reporting quarter. It will be dispatched by registered air mail (15 copies) or by electrical message if not excessively long. At the same time copies will be forwarded by registered mail direct to addressees listed in appendix F, and in the quantities indicated. Specific problems which adversely affect readiness and which are beyond the capability of the

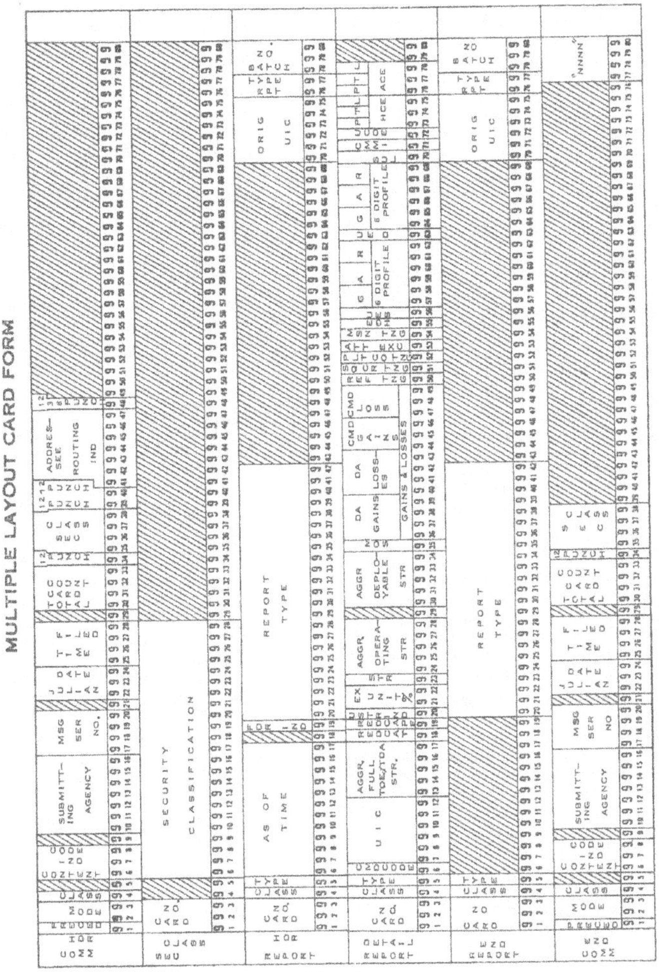

Figure 1.

IMPROVISING A WAR

AR 220-1

major commander to correct will be identified in sufficient detail to permit the Department of the Army to take action. A unit-by-unit listing of problems is not necessary. Listings of personnel by MOS, equipment and repair parts shortages which jeopardize mission accomplishments are required. Discrepancies between REDCAPE and REDCON for major combat units (battalion and larger) require identification and explanation. The current status of training in major combat units will be summarized. Definite command-wide problems or trends will be reported together with the major Army commander's plan for corrective action. Include the extent to which subordinate units have been "zeroed out" or placed into caretaker status due to personnel shortages and projectable recovery dates. Significant developments or improvements within the command in the readiness area should also be listed and explained.

 b. *Personnel section.* This section will include a strength summary, in tabular form, to contain the following: Column A—Command (to include major subordinate command); Column B—Summary of full TOE strengths of all TOE units by identity; Column C—Summary of REDCAT strengths of all TOE units by identity; Column D—Summary of REDCAPE strengths of all TOE units by identity; Column E—TDA strength requirement by identity; Column F—TDA strength authorization by identity; Column G—Command authorized strength by identity (Colm D plus Colm F); Column H—Total accountable strength by identity; Column I—Total operating strength by identity (REDCON strength).

 c. *Logistics section.* This section will include an evaluation of the adequacy or inadequacy of command-wide facilities, funds, equipment asset data, repair parts, tools, technical assistance, and maintenance management. It is emphasized that this section must contain sufficient detailed information for Department of the Army to take expeditious action when required. The following guidance is provided:

 (1) *Facilities.* Identify the installation and/or activity affected by the shortage of facilities and relate how these contribute to reduced readiness. Specifics as to types of facilities will be indicated. Cite Military Construction Appropriation (MCA) number if known. Facility requirements and availability will be reviewed and commented upon as of the 4th fiscal quarter report. These requirements will also be reviewed during the 2d quarter to insure consideration for inclusion of new construction in the next fiscal year budget. Commanders will indicate any additional requirements which develop during the year due to changes in TOE, introduction of new equipment, or mission expansions.

 (2) *Funds.* Include statement of obligation or funding problems affecting readiness. Where shortages exist, specify shortage by budget account.

 (3) *Equipment asset data.*

 (a) Commanders will include a detailed explanation for major items of equipment falling below established equipment objectives command-wide. Items will be listed by line item, noun, authorized level, on hand amounts, quantity short, and requisitioning data for shortages. The explanation will include specific reasons for this condition.

 (b) Commanders will provide a brief analysis of significant problems which cannot be resolved within available resources and which are contributing to a material readiness status that is below established objectives.

 (c) Emphasis will be placed on—
  1. Shortages of equipment that caused excessive use of available equipment.
  2. Low density equipments whose dispersion causes logistical support problems.
  3. Maintenance effort in the application of approved modification work orders.
  4. Abnormal equipment failure.

AR 220-1

5. Overage, obsolete, contingency and training, and non-type classified equipment. (This will include the identification by item and quantity of such equipment on hand.)
6. When conditions indicate future replacements requirements for equipment, the analysis will state the status of current redistribution plans to transfer modern assets to high priority combat units, if applicable.

(4) *Repair parts.* In order that expedited followup actions may be taken, major Army commands will review repair parts shortages reported by subordinate commands and determine those items which can be supplied from command assets. A list of the remaining repair parts shortages considered to be critical to material readiness will be included together with the appropriate command requisition information for these requisitions past due. The list will reflect FSN, noun, quantity, requisition number, estimated delivery date (when known), and last known source of supply (routing identifier). In addition a copy of the list, along with appropriate followup cards (AF cards) in MILSTRIP format, identified to the specific major Army commanders will be air mailed by the major Army commander direct to the commanding officer of the last known source of supply.

(5) *Tools.* Actions in regard to the shortage of tools should be similar to those specified for repair parts shortages. Adequacy of tools must be reviewed when new equipment has been scheduled to the command.

(6) *Technical assistance.* Whenever the lack of technical assistance is a factor detrimental to the materiel readiness posture, relate the shortage of technical assistance to the commodity and/or the specific equipment involved.

(7) *Maintenance management.* Include a statement of problems in maintenance operations, management, and supervision affecting readiness.

(8) Major Army commanders will report the days of supply, stockage objective, and balance on hand by class of supply for authorized reserves (AR 11-11) together with any problems in attaining these levels. The above will also be reported for major subordinate elements of USAREUR and USARPAC.

(9) Details submitted in other Department of the Army or Joint Operational Reporting System reports need not be repeated but will be cross-referenced. Although not required, copies of major command initiated reports or analyses may be included as additional inclosures if appropriate.

Section V. LOGISTICS ANALYSIS OF MAJOR ARMY COMMAND SUMMARY EVALUATION

15. Instructions. USASTRATCOM, Headquarters, U.S. Army Materiel Command, and the commodity commands will receive information copies of Major Army Command Summary Evaluations in accordance with instructions in paragraph 14. The following will then be accomplished:

a. Each commodity command will analyze the equipment and repair parts problems pertinent to its area of responsibility and forward findings to the major commander concerned by the 5th day of the third month following the reporting quarter. Information copies of the findings will be provided Commanding General, U.S. Army Materiel Command, ATTN: AMCOR-RO, Department of the Army, Washington, D.C., 20315; and Deputy Chief of Staff for Logistics, ATTN: MROO, Department of the Army, Washington, D.C., 20310.

b. Headquarters, USAMC will perform an analysis of all commodity command reports and forward findings in five copies to Deputy Chief of Staff for Logistics, ATTN: MROO, by the 25th day of the third month following the reporting quarter.

AR 220-1

APPENDIX A
REDCAT/REDCAPE LEVELS

	C1	C2	C3
Military personnel strength.	Level 1 column (100%) TOE/MTOE. Authorized column TDA/MTDA*.	Level 2 column TOE/MTOE.	Level 3 column TOE/MTOE.
Equipment strength	Level 1 column (100%) TOE/MTOE. Authorized column TDA/MTDA*.	Level 2 column TOE/MTOE.	Level 3 column TOE/MTOE.
Unit deployment (employment) objective under mobilization conditions.	Ready to execute any TOE/MTOE (TDA/MTDA) mission within 24 hours for a sustained period.	Ready to execute any TOE/MTOE mission if allowed 15 days to fill resource shortages. (Can execute TOE/MTOE mission but not for a sustained period.)	Ready to execute any TOE/MTOE mission if allowed 30 days to fill resource shortages and/or complete training. (Can partially execute TOE/MTOE mission for a limited period.)

* REDCAT for TDA units are based on requirements columns o

AR 220-1

APPENDIX B
REDCON CRITERIA

Indicators	C1	C2	C3	C4
PERSONNEL (see app C)				
1. Strength (Block 23, DA Form 2715).	Operating strength not less than 95 percent "full TOE." (Level 1.)	Operating strength not less than 85 percent "full TOE." (Level 1.)	Operating strength not less than 75 percent "full TOE." (Level 1.)	Operating strength less than 75 percent "full TOE." (Level 1).
2. Military Occupational Specialty (Block 35, DA Form 2715).	Not less than 86 percent of "full TOE" strength are personnel in operating strength who are qualified to perform the duties of the position to which assigned.	Not less than 77 percent of "full TOE" strength are personnel in operating strength who are qualified to perform the duties of the position to which assigned.	Not less than 68 percent of "full TOE" strength are personnel in operating strength who are qualified to perform the duties of the position to which assigned.	Less than 68 percent of "full TOE" strength are personnel in operating strength who are qualified to perform duties of the position which assigned.
TRAINING (see para 2, app D) *(Combat, combat support, and combat service support units)*				
3. Refresher Training (para 2a) (Mandatory subjects, arms qualification and physical fitness) (Block 50, DA Form 2715).	90 percent or more of individual refresher requirements accomplished.	85–89 percent of individual refresher training requirements accomplished.	80–84 percent of individual refresher training requirements accomplished.	Less than 80 percent of refresher training requirements accomplished.
4. Squad/Crew Proficiency (para 2b) (Block 51, DA Form 2715).	80 percent or more of all squads and crews specified by full TOE satisfactorily completed annual firing and semiannual nonfiring proficiency tests.	70–79 percent of all squads and crews specified by full TOE satisfactorily completed annual firing and semiannual nonfiring proficiency tests.	60–69 percent of all squads and crews specified by full TOE satisfactorily completed annual firing and semiannual nonfiring proficiency tests.	Less than 60 percent of all squads and crews specified by full TOE satisfactorily completed annual firing and semiannual nonfiring proficiency tests.
5. Unit Proficiency (para 2c) (Block 52, DA Form 2715).	100 percent of all platoons and companies specified by full TOE have satisfactorily accomplished ATT/ORT, no-notice exercises, FTX, and TPI, TSI, or NCE, as applicable.	80–99 percent of all platoons and companies specified by full TOE have satisfactorily accomplished ATT/ORT, no-notice exercises, FTX, and TPI, TSI or NCE, as applicable.	60–79 percent of all platoons and companies specified by full TOE have satisfactorily accomplished ATT/ORT, no-notice exercises, FTX, and TPI, TSI or NCE, as applicable.	Less than 60 percent of all platoons and companies specified by full TOE have satisfactorily accomplished ATT/ORT, no-notice exercises, FTX, and TPI, TSI, or NCE, as applicable.

AR 220-1

Indicators	C1	C2	C3	C4
Separate company, not aggregating results of subordinate elements.	Has satisfactorily completed ATT/ORT, no-notice exercises, FTX, and TPI, TSI, or NCE, as applicable.	In the opinion of the commander, could complete without additional training.	In the opinion of the commander, could complete within 30 days.	In the opinion of the commander, could not complete within 30 days.
6. Field Exercises (para 2d) Battalion (including separate battalions) Division/Separate Brigade/Armored Cavalry Regiment (Block 53, DA Form 2715).	Has satisfactorily completed ATT/ORT, no-notice exercises and FTX. 100 percent of battalion-sized units or higher have satisfactorily completed ATT/ORT, no-notice exercises, and FTX, as applicable.	In the opinion of the commander, could complete without additional training. 80–99 percent of battalion-sized units or higher have satisfactorily completed ATT/ORT, no-notice exercises, and FTX, as applicable.	In the opinion of the commander, could complete within 30 days. 60–79 percent of battalion-sized units or higher have satisfactorily completed ATT/ORT, no-notice exercises, and FTX, as applicable.	In the opinion of the commander, could not complete within 30 days. Less than 60 percent of battalion-sized units or higher have satisfactorily completed ATT/ORT, no-notice exercises and FTX, as applicable.
7. Mission Training (para 2e) (Block 54, DA Form 2715.	45 training days of mission training and maintenance have been scheduled and attended by 90 percent or more of operating strength.	43 training days of mission training and maintenance have been scheduled and attended by 80–89 percent of operating strength.	41 training days of mission training and maintenance have been scheduled and attended by 70–79 percent of operating strength.	Less than 41 training days of mission training and maintenance have been scheduled and attended by less than 70 percent of operating strength.

(Air Defense Missile Units) (see para 3, app D)

3. Refresher Training (para 3a) (Block 50, DA Form 2715).	90 percent or more of individual refresher training requirements accomplished.	85–89 percent of individual refresher training requirements accomplished.	80–84 percent of individual refresher training requirements accomplished.	Less than 80 percent of individual refresher training requirements accomplished.
4. Quarterly Operational Readiness Evaluation (para 3b) (Block 51, DA Form 2715).	10 points or more scored on last four quarterly evaluations.	9 points scored on last four quarterly evaluations.	8 points scored on last four quarterly evaluations.	Less than 8 points scored on last four quarterly evaluations.
5. Air Defense Combat Readiness Training Exercises (para 3c) (Block 52, DA Form 2715).	*Hercules:* Unit participation in at least 120 hours of combat readiness training exercises within past 13 months. *Hawk:* 240 hours	*Hercules:* Unit participation in at least 100 hours of combat readiness training exercises within past 13 months. *Hawk:* 200 hours	*Hercules:* Unit participation in at least 80 hours of combat readiness training exercises within past 13 months. *Hawk:* 160 hours	*Hercules:* Unit participation in less than 80 hours of combat readiness training exercises within past 13 months. *Hawk:* Less than 160 hours.
6. Technical Proficiency (para 3e) Inspection (Block 53, DA Form 2715).	Satisfactory rating on the most recent TPI within 13 months.	In the opinion of the commander, could complete successfully without further training.	In the opinion of the commander, could complete successfully within 30 days.	In the opinion of the commander, could not complete successfully within 30 days.

AR 220-1

Indicators	C1	C2	C3	C4
7. Annual Service Practice (para 3d and e) (Block 54, DA Form 2715).	Satisfactory rating on the most recent annual service practice.	In the opinion of the commander, could complete successfully without further training.	In the opinion of the commander, could complete successfully within 30 days.	In the opinion of the commander, could not complete successfully within 30 days.
		LOGISTICS (see app E)		
8. Equipment on Hand (Block 55, DA Form 2715).	Not less than 90 percent of "full TOE" (level 1) reportable line items at 90 percent fill.	Not less than 90 percent of "full TOE" (level 1) reportable line items at 80 percent fill.	Not less than 90 percent of "full TOE" (level 1) reportable line items at 70 percent fill.	More than 10 percent of "full TOE" (level 1) reportable line items at less than 70 percent fill.
9. Unit Equipment Serviceability (Blocks 56–62, DA Form 2715).	Unit equipment profile not less than 70 20 10.	Unit equipment profile not less than 55 30 15.	Unit equipment profile not less than 40 40 20.	Unit equipment profile less than 40 40 20.
10. Unit Equipment Deployability (Blocks 63–69, DA Form 2715).	Unit equipment profile not less than 70 20 10.	Unit equipment profile not less than 55 30 15.	Unit equipment profile not less than 40 40 20.	Unit equipment profile less than 40 40 20.
11. Unit Loads: (Enter a single unit load REDCON in block 70, DA Form 2715. See appendix E paragraph 5d.)				
Prescribed Load Lists.	0–10 percent of repartable line items at zero balance	11–15 percent of repartable line items at zero balance.	16–20 percent of repartable line items at zero balance.	More than 20 percent of repartable line items at zero balance.
Authorized Stockage.	14 days of supply or more on hand.	10–13 days of supply on hand.	6–9 days of supply on hand.	Less than 6 days of supply on hand.
Class I, III, and V.	Not less than 95 percent of authorized line items on hand at 90 percent fill.	Not less than 90 percent of authorized line items on hand at 90 percent fill.	Not less than 85 percent of authorized line items on hand at 90 percent fill.	More than 15 percent of authorized line items at less than 90 percent fill.
12. Command Maintenance Management Inspection (Block 71, DA Form 2715).	Satisfactory rating on most recent CMMI within 13 months (for 90 percent of subordinate units for battalion size or larger reporting units).	Satisfactory rating for 80 percent of subordinate units for battalion size or larger reporting units on most recent CMMI within 13 months.	Satisfactory rating for 70 percent of subordinate units for battalion size or larger reporting units on most recent CMMI within 13 months.	Unsatisfactory rating for individual unit reporting, or less than 70 percent of subordinate units for battalion size or larger reporting units, on most recent CMMI within 18 months. Unit has not received a CMMI within last 13 months.

22   AGO 6875A

AR 220-1

APPENDIX C
PERSONNEL

Instructions for Preparation of Personnel Section, Unit Readiness Report.

1. **Strength.** *a.* Enter within the area and to the right of Block 23 the information listed below:

Example

	OFF	WO	ENL	AGG
Full TOE strength (blocks 13–17)	29	7	335	371
Authorized strength	24	6	304	334
Accountable strength	26	5	316	347
Operating strength*	22	3	302	327
Deployable strength (CONUS/long tour oversea areas only)	18	3	287	308

* OTSG officers fillers and earmarked AMEDS officers and enlisted personnel will be included in the operating strength.

b. Compute strength status by dividing the operating strength by the full TOE strength.

Example

$$\frac{\text{Operating strength}}{\text{Full TOE strength}} = \frac{327}{371} = 0.881 = 88.1\% \text{ (C2)}$$

c. Compare the percentage obtained to the strength condition indicator and determine your "C" rating.

d. Enter "C" rating in Block 23.

2. **Military Occupational Specialty (MOS).** *a.* Determine the number of personnel authorized by identity (officers, WO, enlisted) and by Military Occupational Specialty Code (MOSC). All five characters of the MOSC prescribed in the authorization document will be used.

b. Determine the number of personnel included in the total operating strength of the unit, by identity and by MOSC. Match them against the authorized spaces.

(1) For this comparison, personnel awarded secondary MOSC (SMOSC), additional MOSC (AMOSC) and personnel with related or other MOSC who are performing duties or being trained or retrained to perform duties to meet the MOSC requirement of the unit will be considered qualified when in the judgment of the unit commander the individual can perform the required duties.

(2) Personnel overstrength in a specific skill in a unit who cannot be utilized as in (1) above, will not be considered. *For example,*

AR 220-1

if a unit is authorized four cooks and has six MOSC qualified cooks assigned, only four of them will be considered as MOSC qualified against the requirement for cooks. However, if the two surplus cooks have a SMOSC of truck driver and they are performing duties as truck drivers they will be considered MOS qualified for this computation provided appropriate vacancies exist.

Example

	Operating strength MOS qualified	Operating strength not MOS qualified
Hq Btry	163	8
A Btry	73	4
B Btry	75	4
	311	16

Total MOS qualified
Full TOE strength $\frac{311}{371} = 0.838 = 83.8\%$ (C2)
(Blocks 18–17)

   c. Enter the percentage obtained in space provided to the right of Block 35.

   d. Compare the percentage obtained to the MOS condition indicator and obtain the "C" rating.

   e. Enter the "C" rating in Block 35.

  3. **Gains/losses.** *a.* Determine the gains and losses to the operating strength of the unit during the reporting quarter.

   b. These data are to be broken down to show to what the gain or loss is attributed, e.g., Department of the Army (replacements, levy, completion of tours, ETS, deaths and desertions) or command (local reassignment, intra-command reassignment).

Example

	Beginning of period	End of period	Gains	losses
Operating strength	325	327	15	13

GAINS		LOSSES	
Department of the Army replacements	12	Rotation	6
Command reassignments	3	ETS	4
		Local reassignment	2
		Command reassignment	1

   c. Enter the above in two columns in the space designated, DA Gains/Losses, and Command Gains/Losses in the area headed by Block 35, DA Form 2715.

Example

DA gains/losses	Command gains/losses
12/10	3/3

AR 220-1

APPENDIX D
TRAINING

1. Unit REDCON for each training readiness indicator in appendix B will be determined as shown below. For units submitting consolidated reports in accordance with paragraph 11a of this regulation, REDCON for each indicator will be computed as shown in paragraphs 2a(2), 2b(4), 2c(3), 2d(5), and 2e(6) below. The overall training REDCON will be the lowest REDCON for any of the indicators.

2. Combat, Combat Support (including AD Artillery Automatic Weapons), and Combat Service Support Units.

   a. Refresher Training—(block 50, DA Form 2715).

   (1) Based on accomplishment of following training by personnel who compose the unit's operating strength and require the training prescribed by applicable regulations:

   (a) Mandatory subjects:

   Character Guidance—One hour per month (AR 600–30)

   Chemical, Biological and Radiological Refresher—As required to maintain proficiency (AR 220–58)

   Civil Affairs—As required to provide an understanding of Civil Affairs matters (AR 350–25)

   Code of Conduct—As required to maintain proficiency (AR 350–30)

   Command Information—One period per week (AR 360–81)

   Military Justice—Three hours (Course B) after 6 months active duty or upon reenlistment (AR 350–212)

   Safeguarding Defense Information—As required to make personnel aware of security responsibilities (AR 380–5)

   Subversion and Espionage Directed Against U.S. Army—Annual Orientation (AR 381–12)

   Survival Evasion and Escape—As required to maintain proficiency (AR 350–225)

   (b) Arms qualification/familiarization annually in accordance with AR 622–5; includes required firing for personnel manning OVE weapons.

   (c) Physical Fitness testing semiannually in accordance with AR 600–9.

   (2) Sample computation for 100 man unit (percentages will be rounded off to nearest whole number):

	Number requiring training	Number successfully completed training
All mandatory subjects	90	60
All arms qualification/familiarization	95	85
Physical fitness	100	90
Total	285	235

$$\frac{235}{285} = 82\%$$

AR 220-1

b. Squad/Crew Proficiency (not applicable to combat service support units) (Block 51, DA Form 2715):
   (1) Based on satisfactory completion of firing proficiency tests within the last 13 months and nonfiring proficiency tests within the last 6 months by the following squads/crews:
   Combat squads (rifle, scout, combat engineer).
   Tank crews.
   Artillery Sections.
   AD Artillery Automatic Weapons Crews.
   Weapons Crews (Firing requirement for OVE weapons is provided for in $a(1)(b)$ above).
   (2) Firing proficiency test requirements for artillery sections and weapons crews may be met by participation in firing tests for parent units. PERSHING battalions may substitute appropriate simulated live firings in lieu of actual firing "within the last 13 months."
   (3) Nonfiring proficiency tests will be based on applicable firing tests adapted to local training areas. Commanders will prepare nonfiring proficiency tests pending publication of outline tests by Department of the Army.
   (4) Sample computation for units submitting consolidated reports (percentages will be rounded off to nearest full number):

Type unit	Total number authorized by TOE	Number satisfactorily completed requirements
Combat Squads	81	75
Tank Crews	60	50
Artillery Sections	18	16
Weapons Crews	72	65
Total	231	206 $\frac{206}{231} = 89\%$

c. Unit Proficiency (Block 52, DA Form 2715):
   (1) Based on satisfactory participation by platoon and company/battery/troop in ATT/ORT, FTX, no-notice exercises and Technical Proficiency Inspection (TPI), Techical Standardization Inspection (TSI), or Nuclear Capability Exercise (NCE) as follows:

Type unit	ATT/ORT	24-hour No-notice exercise	72-hour FTX	TPI, TSI, NCE (when applicable)
Combat and Combat Support:				
* Special Platoons/Sections	w/i 13 months	w/i 6 months	2 w/i 13 months	w/i 13 months
Platoons	w/i 13 months	w/i 6 months	4 w/i 13 months	
Co/Btry/Trp	w/i 13 months	w/i 6 months	4 w/i 13 months	w/i 13 months
Combat Service Support:				
Company	w/i 13 months		2 w/i 13 months	w/i 13 months

   (2) FTX and no-notice exercises requirement may be accomplished by participation in exercises for larger units; no-notice exercises requirements are not intended to interfere with similar activities in certain oversea commands.
   (3) Sample computation for units submitting consolidated reports (percentages will be rounded off to the nearest whole number):

AR 220-1

Type unit	Number specified by full TOE	Number satisfactorily completed requirements
Combat and Combat Support:		
Special Platoons/Sections	50	45
Platoon	81	78
Co/Btry/Trp	30	27
Combat Service Support:		
Company	10	9
Total	171	159

$$\frac{159}{171} = 93\%$$

(4) When ratings are based on the commander's opinion of the time required to attain C1, the training status of the unit rather than available resources or facilities will be the basis for such ratings.

(5) Company or equivalent-sized units whose reports are not consolidated at battalion level will determine REDCON based on the applicable portions of the instructions in (1) through (4) above.

(6) Pending publication of outline tests by Department of the Army, commanders will prepare ATT-ORT for special sections not published by Department of the Army.

* Special Platoon/Sections are DAVY CROCKETT Sections, ADM Platoons, Communication Platoons, Ground Surveillance Sections and REDEYE Sections.

d. Field Exercises: (Not applicable to separate companies) (Block 53, DA Form 2715):

(1) Based on satisfactory completion of ATT/ORT, no-notice exercises and FTX as applicable, by battalion or larger-sized units as follows:

Type unit	ATT/ORT	72-hour FTX	24-hour No-notice exercise	Brigade exercise	Division exercise
Battalion Squadron		1 w/i 18 months	1 w/i 6 months	1 w/i 6 months		
Brigade/Armored Cavalry Regiment				1 w/i 18 months	1 w/i 18 months
Division					1 w/i 18 months

(2) FTX requirements may be met by participation in FTX for larger units.

(3) Combat Service Support Units must have participated in at least one FTX of at least 72-hour duration within the last 13 months.

(4) Combat Service Support Units will be administered ATT/ORT as part of FTX conducted for a supported unit.

(5) Sample computation for units submitting consolidated reports (percentages will be rounded off to the nearest whole number):

Type unit	Number authorized	Number satisfactorily completed requirements (C1 rating for Bn and Sqdn)
Battalion/Squadron	18	16
Brigade	3	3
Division	1	1
Total	22	20

$$\frac{20}{22} = 91\%$$

(6) When ratings are based on the commander's opinion of the time required to attain C1, the training status of the unit rather than available resources or facilities will be the basis for such ratings.

AR 220-1

  e. Mission Training (Block 54, DA Form 2715):

   (1) Based on scheduling of, and attendance at, mission training and maintenance conducted in accordance with AR 350-1 which, as a guide, provides for 45 training days of mission training and maintenance per quarter, or an average of 3½ days per week. Allowance may be made in ratings to compensate for Christmas holiday scheduling.

   (2) Mission training is training conducted at squad or equivalent level or higher to prepare units to carry out operational missions.

   (3) Operating strength is accountable strength less intransit and attached strength (see para 4g, AR 220-1).

   (4) Personnel performing TOE assigned administrative and logistical support duties will be credited with attendance at mission training; personnel performing unit details, i.e., KP, guard, post support, will not be so credited.

   (5) Daily status reflecting the number of personnel at training and performing TOE assigned administrative and logistical support duties, will be used as a basis for computations.

   (6) REDCON for units submitting consolidated reports will be the lowest C rating included in 90 percent of subordinate reporting elements.

 3. Air Defense Missile Units. (Air defense automatic weapons units will report under the indicators provided for combat support units.)

  a. Refresher Training (Block 50, DA Form 2715):

   (1) Based on accomplishment of following training by personnel who compose the unit's operating strength and require the training prescribed by applicable regulations:

    (a) Mandatory subjects:

     Character Guidance—One hour per month (AR 600-30)

     Chemical, Biological, and Radiological Refresher—As required to maintain proficiency (AR 220-58)

     Civil Affairs—As required to provide an understanding of Civil Affairs matters (AR 350-25)

     Code of Conduct—As required to maintain proficiency (AR 350-30)

     Command Information—One period per week (AR 360-81)

     Military Justice—Three hours (Course B) after 6 months active duty or upon reenlistment (AR 350-212)

     Safeguarding Defense Information—As required to make personnel aware of security responsibilities (AR 380-5)

     Subversion and Espionage Directed Against U.S. Army—Annual orientation (AR 381-12)

     Survival Evasion and Escape—As required to maintain proficiency (AR 350-225)

    (b) Arms qualification/familiarization in accordance with AR 622-5 for Active Army personnel and Appendix XVIII, Annex AA, CONARC Regulation 350-1 for National Guard personnel; includes required firing for personnel manning OVE weapons.

    (c) Physical fitness testing in accordance with AR 600-9 for Active Army personnel and Section 1, Annex AA, CONARC Regulation 350-1 for National Guard personnel.

AR 220-1

	Number requiring training	Number accomplishing training
(2) Sample computation:		
Mandatory subjects	90	60
Arms qualification/familiarization	95	85
Physical fitness	100	90
Total	285	235 $\frac{235}{285} = 82\%$

 b. Quarterly Operational Readiness Evaluation (Block 51, DA Form 2715):
  (1) Based on the total points scored in the last four quarterly operational readiness evaluations.
  (2) Each quarterly evaluation conducted by group (defense in ARADCOM) or higher headquarters has a value of 3 points allocated as follows:
   (*a*) 1 point for satisfactory overall rating.
   (*b*) 1 point for satisfactory crew performance in the fire control area.
   (*c*) 1 point for satisfactory crew performance in the launching area.

 c. Air Defense Combat Readiness Training Exercises consist of live flying exercises (ADE), FTX, mobility training, and guided missile system simulator training exercises (Block 52, DA Form 2715).

 d. Annual Service Practice is required once each fiscal year. In oversea commands, in-theater ORT within 13 months, utilizing the appropriate missile system simulator, fulfills this requirement. ASP will be conducted within 6 months of an in-theater ORT (Block 54, DA Form 2715).

 e. When ratings are based on the commander's opinion of the time required to attain C1, the training status of the unit rather than available resources or facilities will be the basis for such ratings.

AR 220-1

APPENDIX E
LOGISTICS

1. Equipment on hand. For equipment on hand (Block 55), standards are stated as "not less than a given percentage of reportable line items at a given percentage of fill." Only equipment type classified as Standard A, B or Limited Production (P) and identified in AR 711-140 as essential to the field Army mission Reportable Item Control Code (RICC-1) line items will be reported. Computation is as follows: Determine equipment to be considered by utilizing the TOE/MTOE for authorization and AR 711-140 for line items (RICC-1) to be reported. For TDA units designated to report under this regulation, the TDA proponent will identify line items which are mission essential. Communications Security Equipment listed in the DA Form 2406 column of AR 750-38 (C) will be reported. For equipment (type classified A, B, or limited production) issued in lieu of authorized reportable items—

  a. It is reportable if it has similar operating characteristics and is capable of performing the combat mission requirement of the TOE authorized item.

  b. It is reportable if issued in other than a one-for-one basis, using the quantity of the item that was substituted in the computation of the rating; e.g., if two 5 KW generators are issued as an adequate substitute for one 10 KW generator, the possession of two 5 KW generators will be equated to the possession of one 10 KW generator.

  c. It is not reportable if it does not have similar operating characteristics or will not perform the combat mission requirement of the authorized item; e.g., one 5 KW generator normally would not be considered as a substitute for a 10 KW generator.

  d. Report those items issued in lieu of authorized reportable RICC-1 line items. If the "in-lieu" of item is not a RICC-1 reportable item, it will be considered as RICC-1 and/or mission essential and reported accordingly. If an RICC-1 item is held in lieu of nonreportable line items as authorized in the TOE/MTOE, the item will not be included in equipment on hand computations.

  e. Report line items that are RICC-1 and that make up part of a system if listed separately in the TOE. Line items that are RICC-1 and that are part of a system as authorized in the TOE, will be reported according to the reportable status of the system.

  f. Enter to the right of Block 55 the data upon which the REDCON was computed in a five-number sequence. The first number to be the number of reportable lines being reported upon followed by the number of lines meeting C1, C2, C3, and C4 level in that sequence with each number being separated by a slash (e.g., 329/300/20/0/9).

2. Equipment serviceability and deployability. a. *Equipment condition.* The condition of selected items of equipment are described as one of the following categories as established by ESC scores:

  (1) *GREEN.* Equipment free of condition that would limit the reliable performance of its primary mission for a period of 90 days of operation.

AR 220-1

(2) *AMBER.* Operationally ready equipment that possesses a limiting factor(s) which may curtail a reliable performance of its primary mission for a period of 90 days of operation.

(3) *RED.* Equipment unable to perform its primary mission immediately or possessing an unacceptable reliability for sustained performance (90 days) of its primary mission.

b. *General instructions.*

(1) All equipment type-classified Standard A, B or Limited Production (P) listed in the DA Form 2406 column of Appendix III, TM 38-750 will be counted as assets on hand for reporting purposes. Communications security equipment listed in the DA Form 2406 column of AR 750-38 (C) will be reported.

   (a) Items listed in the TOE/MTOE as developmental type (DT) will not be considered in computing equipment authorized or on hand.

   (b) "In-lieu" of items issued that are type classified Standard A, B, or Limited Production, and contain similar operational characteristics and combat capabilities as the authorized item will be considered as on hand for profiling purposes. Reportable items on hand in lieu of other items on an other than one-for-one basis will be reported as individual items. In computing the deployability profile the authorized amount will be adjusted accordingly.

(2) Equipment condition is determined by checking the item against the standards listed in the applicable Equipment Serviceability Criteria (ESC). ESCs will be considered current when they have been performed within the 90-day period preceding the "as of" reporting date provided the equipment log book has no subsequent entries which invalidate that ESC. The equipment will be placed in applicable category (GREEN, AMBER, or RED) in accordance with the results of evaluation. If an ESC has not been published for a reportable item (including "in-lieu" of), and the item will perform its primary mission, it will be rated GREEN; if the item cannot perform its primary mission by virtue of its condition (unapplied urgent MWO or inoperative) it will be rated RED.

(3) Equipment will be classified RED when one or more urgent modification work orders have not been applied.

(4) Equipment in maintenance above organizational level, for repair and return to the reporting unit, will be considered on hand and scored RED. Equipment in organizational maintenance and returnable within 24 hours will be considered as on hand and scored in accordance with the applicable ESC when computing the profile.

(5) Equipment in administrative storage.

   (a) Equipment is considered to be in administrative storage when it is on the property account of the reporting unit and is stored in accordance with TB ORD 1045, Administrative Storage of Army Vehicles. Preservation, storage and inspection guidance is contained in TM 38-450.

   (b) Equipment will not be placed in storage in RED condition.

   (c) Stored equipment will be considered as on hand if it can be made available to the unit within 24 hours. If equipment cannot be reassembled or available to the unit within 24 hours it will be categorized RED.

(6) Multiple aspect equipment such as a tank which has integral subsystems, issued under a single FSN (automotive, armament, fire control, and communication), will be considered as a complete system for the determination of equipment profiles. Therefore, for the tank to be GREEN, all subsystems must be GREEN.

AR 220-1

(7) Combinations of separately authorized or issued configurations (FSNs) that are dependent upon each other for an effective operation will be rated as a single system when computing equipment deployability profiles. (Radios, authorized or issued separately for mounting in the tank, create a tank/radio combination; or, the combination of a truck/radio shelter/radio set/trailer and generator which are authorized or issued for the purpose of being combined for operations; or a ¼-ton truck which mounts a separately issued recoilless rifle.) For a system to be rated GREEN under deployability profiling, all separately issued configurations must be GREEN. If the generator in the truck/radio shelter/radio set/trailer and generator combination is RED, then the entire combination is RED. For missile systems, see paragraph 4.

c. *Equipment profile.* An equipment profile is a 6-digit number which describes in percentages the condition of a group of like items. It is developed from the scores resulting from the application of the ESC. A profile is stated in terms of GREEN, AMBER, and RED percentages of a quantity. (For missile systems, the profile is a 6-digit number which describes the operational availability of the system. The missile system profile is stated in terms of GREEN, AMBER, and RED percentages of system operational time.) An example of the profile computation follows:

Item	Total	GREEN	AMBER	RED
Truck, cargo, 2½-ton	50	35	10	5

Computation		
Color %	$\dfrac{\text{Quantity by Color}}{\text{Total Quantity}}$	$\times\ 100$
GREEN %	$\dfrac{35}{50} \times 100$	$= 70\%$
AMBER %	$\dfrac{10}{50} \times 100$	$= 20\%$
RED %	$\dfrac{5}{50} \times 100$	$= 10\%$

(Profile is 70 20 10)

d. *Unit equipment profile.* A unit equipment profile is a collective term describing the overall level of serviceability/deployability of selected unlike items in a unit. This profile is a 6-digit number denoting GREEN, AMBER, and RED in percentages. Utilization of unit equipment profiles in readiness reporting under this regulation provides for two types; serviceability profile and deployability profile.

e. *Serviceability profile (Block 56):*

(1) This profile depicts the readiness of the unit with respect to the condition of the unit's on hand reportable equipment. Specifically, the equipment serviceability profile measures the materiel readiness of Standard A, B, and Limited Production equipment on hand regardless of authorization.

(2) Contingency and training (C&T), obsolete (OBS), non-type classified (N) equipment shortages and equipment on loan that cannot be returned to the owning unit within 24 hours will be excluded from the computation of this profile.

(3) Equipment borrowed which cannot be returned to the owning unit within 24 hours will be considered as on hand by the borrowing unit and reported.

(4) Equipment under control of the owning organization, but is on a TDY or training mission and returnable to the owning organization will be included in the profile.

f. *Equipment deployability profile (Block 63).*

AR 220-1

(1) This profile depicts the readiness for deployment of the reporting unit with respect to the availability and condition of items authorized by TOE/MTOE or TDA/MTDA. Contingency and training, obsolete or non-type classified equipment on hand in the unit will be classified RED in the computation of this profile.

(2) In computing this profile, TOE/MTOE equipment shortages will be scored as RED (unless an acceptable substitute item is issued "in-lieu" of, per paragraph 2b(1)(b) above).

(3) Loaned or TDY equipment, outside the operational control of the reporting unit and not returnable to the reporting unit within 24 hours will be considered short and scored as RED.

(4) Borrowed or hand receipt equipment will not be considered.

g. *Example of profile computation.*

Item	Authorized	On hand	GREEN	AMBER	RED (ESC score)	Short
Truck, ¼ ton	125	100	70	20	10	25
Truck, Cargo 2½ ton	100	75	60	10	5	25
Helicopter, Utility	10	10	0	0	10	0
Tank, Combat Medium	100	100	70	20	10	0
Radio Set	100	100	85	10	5	0
Airplane, Observation	10	10	0	5	5	0
Generator, 5 KW *	0	5	5	0	0	0
Total	445	400	290	65	45	50

* Not included in Equipment Deployability Profile below.

Equipment Serviceability Profile:

$$\frac{\text{Color}}{\text{On hand}} \times 100$$

GREEN % $\frac{290}{400} \times 100 = 73\%$

AMBER % $\frac{65}{400} \times 100 = 16\%$

RED % $\frac{45}{400} \times 100 = 11\%$

(Serviceability Profile is 73 16 11) (Blocks 57 to 62)

Equipment Deployability Profile:

$$\frac{\text{Color}}{\text{TOE/MTOE/Authorized}} \times 100$$

GREEN % $\frac{285}{445} \times 100 = 64\%$

AMBER % $\frac{65}{445} \times 100 = 15\%$

RED % $\frac{95}{445} \times 100 = 21\%$

(Deployability Profile is 64 15 21) (Blocks 64 to 69)

h. *Profile format.* The percentage of GREEN, AMBER, and RED in a profile totals 100 percent. Five percent is written 05 to maintain the 6-digit profile. To minimize error, 100 percent GREEN will be shown as 990000, 100 percent AMBER as 009900, and 100 percent RED as 000099.

3. **Condition of equipment.** Profiles are used to establish the Readiness Condition (RED-CON) of a unit's equipment.

a. Minimum Equipment Profiles are (app B)—

	GREEN	AMBER	RED	C rating
	70%	20%	10%	C1
	55%	30%	15%	C2
	40%	40%	20%	C3
(less than)	40%	40%	20%	C4

AR 220-1

b. C ratings are determined from the GREEN and RED portions of the unit equipment profiles. To qualify in the C ratings above, the unit must meet the minimum GREEN portion and not exceed RED portion. *Examples*—

GREEN	AMBER	RED	
71%	16%	*13%	C2 rating
*50%	40%	10%	C3 rating

* Determinant factor.

4. **Profile condition of equipment for guided missile units.** a. Nonfire units (HQ and service-type units) will determine profiles in the manner outlined in paragraphs 2 and 3.

b. Guided missile fire units will develop two profiles for equipment as follows:

(1) Equipment profiles will be computed for conventional equipment as prescribed in paragraphs 2 and 3. For a guided missile unit, conventional equipment is identified as a reportable item not included in primary equipment category 600000 (app III, TM 38-750). This profile will be entered in blocks 64 through 69 (Deployability Profile), DA Form 2715. (For fixed air defense units within the United States see f below.)

(2) A missile system availability indicator for primary equipment category 600000 items will be computed over the reporting period as outlined below. This profile will be entered in blocks 57 through 62 (Serviceability Profile), DA Form 2715.

c. The following criteria will be used to determine readiness condition (REDCON) for missile systems:

(1) *Surface to air missiles.* Only system downtime for a fire unit in excess of 10 minutes will be considered nonoperational time. The fire unit includes a double battery.

(a) GREEN (time). The missile system is fully operational with 100 percent acquisition, tracking, and computer capabilities and capable of launching missiles. This includes Range Only Radar (ROR) or Target Range Radar (TRR) as applicable. At least one-half of the units' assigned missiles with associated launching equipment must be operational. All systems equipment must be capable of being operated on an available tactical power source.

(b) AMBER (time). Missile system is less than GREEN but has an acceptable minimum tactical battery availability as follows:

1. *NIKE-HERCULES.* The fire unit must have as a minimum—
   (a) An acquisition capability 100 percent operational.
   (b) All computing and missile tracking capability 100 percent operational.
   (c) A target tracking capability 100 percent operational.
   (d) Fifty percent of launchers, launcher control, and associated materiel operational.
   (e) Fifty percent of assigned missiles operational and capable of being launched on operational equipment cited above.
   (f) Operational equipment must be capable of being operated on an available tactical power source.

2. *HAWK.* The fire unit must have as a minimum—
   (a) The CW acquisition radar 100 percent operational.
   (b) Either the BCC or the AFCC 100 percent operational.
   (c) One of the illuminators 100 percent operational.
   (d) Fifty percent of launchers and associated materiel operational (minimum of one loader operational).

AR 220-1

(e) Operational equipment must be capable of being operated on an available tactical power source.
(c) *RED* (*time*). System fails to meet the minimum criteria for AMBER.
(2) *Surface to surface guided missiles.* Nonoperational time and criteria for PERSHING and nonoperational time for SERGEANT are published periodically in DA message form (CONFIDENTIAL). Criteria for SERGEANT follows:
(a) *GREEN* (*time*). The fire unit must have as a minimum—
   1. All missile system ground equipment, including launcher, 100 percent operational.
   2. The assigned missiles 100 percent operational and capable of being launched on operational launchers indicated above.
(b) *AMBER* (*time*). No AMBER condition exists under this criterion.
(c) *RED* (*time*). System fails to meet the minimum criteria for GREEN above.

d. Missile system indicator is a 6-digit number showing the percentage of time the system was in a GREEN, AMBER, and RED condition during the reporting period by considering the criteria in *c* above.

(1) The first two digits (GREEN) represent the percentage of time the system was fully operational during the reporting period.
(2) The second two digits (AMBER) represent the percentage of time the system maintained an acceptable minimum availability during the reporting period.
(3) The third two digits (RED) represent the percentage of time the system was not operable during the reporting period.

e. To determine the REDCON for serviceability of items of missile system equipment, during the reporting period, the GREEN and AMBER digits are added and the availability (REDCON) of equipment is determined as follows:

(1) C1—Equipment available 85 percent or more of the time.
(2) C2—Equipment aavilable 75 percent but less than 85 percent of the time.
(3) C3—Equipment available 65 percent but less than 75 percent of the time.
(4) C4—Equipment available less than 65 percent of the time.

f. The unit equipment deployability profile on conventional equipment and the missile system availability indicator are both reportable for missile fire units. Exception to reporting on conventional equipment is granted to fixed air defense units within the United States.

5. Unit loads. REDCON (C rating) will be determined by using the percentage standards in indicator 10, Appendix B, and applying the weighting factors as shown in *d* below.

a. Class I, III, Basic (Class V). Assets earmarked for a unit in CONUS will be considered on hand if they can be made available to the unit prior to deployment time (app A).

b. Prescribed Load Lists (PLL). The PLL is complied in accordance with paragraph 6 of AR 735-35. The REDCON (C rating) is determined by the percent of lines of mission essential repair parts contained on the PLL which are at zero balance at the end of the reporting period. The quantity of mission essential repair parts is based on prescribed allowance of those items as increased based on demand. Mission essential repair parts are those which are essential for maintenance of a mission essential end item or system in a state of combat readiness and those additional repair parts required for installation of the essential item. The mission essential repair parts lists will be recommended by the unit commander and approved under the same procedure as the PLL under AR 735-35. Higher commanders will conduct reviews of the list of mission

AR 220-1

essential repair parts to determine the validity and promote compatibility between similar units so far as practical. For missile systems, where a prescribed allowance is published, the REDCON (C rating) will be determined by the percent of those prescribed lines that are at zero balance at the end of the reporting period. The total number of mission essential PLL lines authorized and the number at zero balance will be shown to the right of the single unit load indicator (Block 70) on the DA Form 2715 (e.g., PLL 800/100).

c. Authorized Stockage Lists (ASL). REDCON (C ratings) are determined by the average number of days of supply, including the safety level, on hand as of the last day of the reporting period. Following is an example:

Days of supply level	Prescribed factor	ASL line	Factored supply days
Zero days	0	5	0
1-5 days	3	15	45
6-13 days	10	45	450
14 days/more	15	35	525
Total		100	1020

*Average days of supply— $\frac{1020}{100} = 10.2$ or 10

* The average number of days is a resulting weighted figure obtained by applying the prescribed factor times the line items reported at that supply level; added and divided by the total number of line items in the ASL. Round off to the nearest whole number (if the average days of supply is 13.5 or higher, the days of supply will be considered 14). The data as to number of reportable lines and number of lines at each level of supply will be shown to the right of the single unit load indicator (Block 70) of DA Form 2715 (e.g., ASL 10,000/3,000/1000/500/500).

d. Single Unit Load REDCON.

(1) To determine a meaningful overall REDCON, the unit loads in Section C, DA Form 2715, which primarily reflect a units' capacity to conduct sustained operations, will be weighted for a single Unit Load REDCON.

(2) Method.

(a) Each unit load will be computed as prescribed in appendix B.

(b) Following these computations, the following weighting will be applied to them:

	Class I	Class III	PLL	ASL*	Basic (CL V)
REDCON 1	.1	.1	.3	.3	.2
REDCON 2	.2	.2	.6	.6	.4
REDCON 3	.3	.3	.9	.9	.6
REDCON 4	.4	.4	1.2	1.2	.8

* Units not authorized an ASL will double the PLL weight factor.

(c) Total the REDCON for each class of supply to arrive at single unit load REDCON.

Example
Reported REDCON

Reporting unit	Class I	Class III	PLL	ASL	Basic (CL V)	Total	Single unit load REDCON
Unit A	C1 = .1	C1 = .1	C1 = .3	C1 = .3	C1 = .2	1.0	C1
*Unit B	C1 = .1	C1 = .1	C4 = 2.4	N/A	C1 = .2	2.8	C3
Unit C	C1 = .1	C1 = .1	C3 = .9	C3 = .9	C2 = .4	2.4	C2
Unit D	C3 = .3	C2 = .2	C4 = 1.2	C4 = 1.2	C3 = .6	3.5	C4

* Not authorized an ASL.

(d) Enter single unit load REDCON in block 70 and consider it in establishment of overall unit REDCON.

AGO 6875A   37

AR 220-1

(e) To the right of block 70, indicate the REDCON computations for each element of the single unit load (e.g., $\frac{\text{CLI}}{\text{C2}} \quad \frac{\text{CLIII}}{\text{C1}} \quad \frac{\text{PLL}}{\text{C4}} \quad \frac{\text{ASL}}{\text{N/A}} \quad \frac{\text{BASIC}}{\text{C1}}$).

6. Consolidation of readiness reports. Specified reporting units will consolidate data from subordinate units to determine appropriate REDCON ratings.

    a. Consolidated readiness condition ratings for equipment on hand, equipment serviceability, and equipment deployability will be accomplished by compiling basic data of organic units. Reporting units will compute percentages and determine resulting REDCON rating by using condition indicators in appendix B. *Example:*

      (1) Organic units submit materiel readiness basic data to consolidating commands.

      (2) Commands consolidate equipment data to obtain totals of items authorized, on hand, and their status (GREEN, AMBER, RED).

      (3) Equipment on hand REDCON rating will be determined from the authorization and on hand status of reportable equipment lines of all organic elements. Back up data will be indicated as required by paragraph 1*f*.

      (4) Compute serviceability and deployability profiles (information pertaining to the deployability profile can be shown in the space adjacent to block 71).

      (5) Determine REDCON ratings.

    b. The computation of the readiness condition (REDCON) rating to determine the single unit load on a consolidated basis will be an average of REDCON ratings of each element (class of supply) of subordinate unit reports. *Example:*

      (1) Assume 20 subordinate units constitute the consolidating command. (This example applies to each class of supply or type unit load.)

      (2) The REDCON rating distribution is C1—3; C2—6; C3—7; and C4—4.

      (3) Each REDCON is multiplied by the number of units in each of the REDCON ratings and then totaled.

$$1 \times 3 = 3$$
$$2 \times 6 = 12$$
$$3 \times 7 = 21$$
$$4 \times 4 = \underline{16}$$
$$52 \text{ Total}$$

      (4) The total of the REDCON ratings is divided by the total number of reporting units.

$$\frac{52}{20} = 2.6 \text{ (REDCON C3)}$$

      (5) The consolidated REDCON is rounded off to the next higher whole number if the fraction is .5 or higher and to the next lower whole number if the fraction is .4 or less. Each element of the unit load is assigned the applicable weight factor in paragraph 5*d* to determine the single unit load REDCON.

      (6) When a unit such as a maintenance battalion of a division reports the unit loads, all supplies held by the forward support companies including ASL, will be included in the battalion report. Computation for the battalion report follows the procedure for consolidated reports.

      (7) The total cumulative number of PLL lines which the subordinate units used to determine their REDCON and cumulative lines at zero balance will be indicated to the right of block 70 (e.g., PLL 12,500/3000).

AR 220-1

(8) The total cumulative number of ASL lines which the subordinate units used to determine their REDCON and cumulative lines at each level of days of supply will be indicated to the right of block 70 (e.g., ASL 6000/4000/1000/500/500).

(9) To the right of block 70, indicate the computed REDCON for each element of the single unit load REDCON (e.g., $\frac{\text{CLI}}{\text{C1}}$ $\frac{\text{CLIII}}{\text{C1}}$ $\frac{\text{PLL}}{\text{C2}}$ $\frac{\text{ASL}}{\text{C3}}$ $\frac{\text{BASIC}}{\text{C1}}$).

7. Command Maintenance Management Inspections (CMMI), (Block 71). This inspection provides an indication of the status of unit materiel readiness and effectiveness of the overall maintenance program to include shop operations, tools and test equipment, personnel, training, records and reports, repair parts supply, publications, and facilities.

a. Battalion size or larger reporting units will consolidate CMMI ratings of subordinate elements and compute the satisfactory percentage for its command. The REDCON C rating is determined by using condition indicator 12, appendix B.

b. Separate reporting units that do not have subordinate elements and which are inspected individually will be rated C1 if satisfactory or C4 if unsatisfactory. Other C ratings are not applicable in this instance.

AR 220-1

APPENDIX F
ADDRESSEES FOR COMMANDERS SUMMARY EVALUATIONS

	Headquarters	Number of copies
1.	Commanding General U.S. Army Material Command ATTN: AMCOR-RO Washington, D.C., 20315	2
2.	Commanding General U.S. Army Mobility Equipment Command ATTN: AMSME-MXA 4300 Goodfellow Boulevard St. Louis, Mo., 63120	4
3.	Commanding General U.S. Army Tank-Automotive Command ATTN: AMSMO-MRO Detroit Arsenal Warren, Mich., 48090	6
4.	Commanding General U.S. Army Missile Command ATTN: AMSMI-SM Redstone Arsenal, Ala., 35809	6
5.	Commanding General U.S. Army Weapons Command ATTN: AMSWE-SM Rock Island Arsenal Rock Island, Ill., 61202	4
6.	Commanding General U.S. Army Munitions Command ATTN: AMSMU-OR Picatinny Arsenal Dover, N.J., 07801	1
7.	Commanding General U.S. Army Ammunition Procurement and Supply Agency ATTN: SMUAP-QXM Joliet, Ill., 60431	3
8.	Commanding General U.S. Army Electronics Command Directorate of Material Readiness ATTN. AMSEL-MR/P-OP1 225 S. 18th Street Philadelphia, Pa., 19103	3

AR 220-1

Headquarters

		Number of copies
9.	Commanding General U.S. Army Electronic Command Directorate of Material Readiness ATTN: AMSEL-MR-(NMP)-MT Fort Monmouth, N.J., 07703	1
10.	Commanding General U.S. Army Aviation Material Command ATTN: AMSAV-CRA P.O. Box 209 St. Louis, Mo., 63166	3
11.	Commanding Officer Lexington-Blue Grass Army Depot ATTN: SSMLB-LDC Lexington, Ky., 40507	2
12.	Commanding General U.S. Army Strategic Communications Command ATTN: SCCCM-OR Washington, D.C., 20315	1

AR 220-1

APPENDIX G
REFERENCES

The following list of publications constitutes a minimum requirement for preparation of unit readiness reports and commanders summary evaluations:

1. **Personnel.**
   - AR 335-60
   - AR 611-101
   - (C) AR 611-102
   - AR 611-112
   - (C) AR 611-113
   - AR 611-201
   - (C) AR 611-202

2. **Training and miscellaneous.**
   - AR 11-15
   - AR 18-50
   - (S) AR 18-50-10
   - AR 220-58
   - AR 310-31
   - AR 310-44
   - AR 350-1
   - AR 350-25
   - AR 350-30
   - AR 350-212
   - AR 350-225
   - AR 360-81
   - AR 380-5
   - AR 381-12
   - AR 600-9
   - AR 600-30
   - AR 622-5
   - JANAP 128

3. **Logistics.**
   - (S) AR 11-11
   - AR 11-14
   - TM 38-450
   - TM 380-750
   - AR 380-6
   - AR 380-40
   - AR 700-20
   - SB 700-20
   - AR 711-5
   - AR 711-140
   - AR 725-50
   - AR 735-35
   - AR 750-1
   - AR 750-5
   - AR 750-8
   - AR 750-38
   - TB ORD 1045

(ODCSOPS)

AR 220-1

By Order of the Secretary of the Army:

HAROLD K. JOHNSON,
General, United States Army,
Chief of Staff.

Official:
KENNETH G. WICKHAM,
Major General, United States Army,
The Adjutant General.

Distribution:
To be distributed in accordance with DA Form 12-9 requirements for Administration:
Active Army: A.   *NG:* **D** Plus "On Site" Missile Units (2).   *USAR:* None.

☆U.S. Government Printing Office: 1967—250-508/6875A

www.ingramcontent.com/pod-product-compliance
Lightning Source LLC
Chambersburg PA
CBHW061646040426
42446CB00010B/1606